FUN WITH FOOD TODDLER COOKBOOK

Fun with Food

TODDLER COOKBOOK

Activities and Recipes to Play and Eat

YAFFI LVOVA, RDN

PHOTOGRAPHY BY ANNIE MARTIN

ILLUSTRATIONS BY DENISE HOLMES

ROCKRIDGE PRESS

Interior and Cover Designer: Elizabeth Zuhl
Art Producer: Janice Ackerman
Editor: Laura Apperson
Production Editor: Rachel Taenzler

Photography © 2020 Annie Martin. Food styling by Nadine Page.

Illustrations © 2020 Denise Holmes.

Author Photo: Crystal Hollman of Crystal Clear Photography: CrystalClearPhotographyAZ.com/author/admin/

ISBN: Print 978-1-64876-003-7 | eBook 978-1-64739-572-8

R0

This book is dedicated
to Little Chef. Eat joyfully,
grow strong, learn
constantly, and, most of
all, laugh often.

Contents

Tropical
Blended
Popsicles
PAGE 121

Introduction

Hi!

I'm Yaffi Lvova, Registered Dietitian Nutritionist and owner of Baby Bloom Nutrition® and Toddler Test Kitchen™.

I've been cooking with my own kids since they were able to face forward in a baby carrier. Along the way, I learned about all the benefits of cooking with kids. I learned how kneading challah dough exposed them to different textures, while helping advance their gross motor skills and introducing them to their rich heritage. I learned that cooking together is a valuable bonding experience between parent and child. The child learns to experience the complete sensory activity that is food, while the parent momentarily travels back to a time of innocence by experiencing food through the wonder of the child's eyes.

Toddler Test Kitchen™ started off as a fun cooking class for young children at a local museum but quickly evolved into much more. What began as a small class turned into a larger culinary adventure where children learned how to appreciate colors, textures, and flavors that were previously distasteful to them. The biggest surprise to me, and my greatest joy in teaching, has been watching the parents' joy as they learned how capable their small child was, both in physical skill and in willingness to adopt an adventurous outlook at the table.

In my five years of teaching this class, I've seen palates expand and parents relax, and, most importantly, I've seen shared smiles take the place of anxiety and frustration.

In this book, I'll share the many benefits of adding fun to your food at the table, in the kitchen, and even in the garden. I'll guide you through activities and recipes to help you bring joy to your table and encourage a healthy relationship with food in your child. And you know what? It might also benefit your own relationship with food in the process.

Got your chef's hat on? Let's get started!

Muffin Coloring

PAGE 35
▼

Morning Glory Muffins
PAGE 33

CHAPTER ONE

Playing and Cooking in the Kitchen

Ready to bring your child into the kitchen for some fun? I know you're concerned about *the mess*, the time it will take, *the mess*, the frustration, and, most importantly, *the mess*. We can take this step-by-step. The critical thing is that you, the parent or caregiver, feel confident and comfortable. Then the fun can begin.

1

Successful Cooking with Your Toddler

Cooking isn't just a fun and engaging activity that results in something delicious—there are some sneaky benefits, too. Your toddler will hone their fine and gross motor skills, improve their language skills, and experience social and emotional development, all in the kitchen! As your toddler is given safe and age-appropriate control in meal preparation, their confidence will grow. And that benefits so many different and essential areas of development.

Graduating from ABCs

When preparing food with toddlers, verbal repetition is important. This goes over very well for the home chef who naturally talks to themself while cooking. (No, I'm not referring to myself . . .) When we verbalize amounts, ingredients, and the order of steps, we are teaching language skills without even knowing it. Children watch, listen, and absorb the sounds we make and the cadence of our speech patterns, and they begin to associate those sounds with specific ingredients. Engage in conversation with your child throughout the process, even if they are not yet at an age when they can respond, because children are such sponges.

Each small success in the kitchen provides a boost of confidence that will serve toddlers well as they get older. They will naturally be more comfortable overcoming social and academic hurdles both big and small. For the littlest chefs, that kitchen success might be dumping half a cup of flour into a mixing bowl. For the more advanced crowd, that might mean using a cookie cutter or peeling a carrot.

The experience of spending joyful time exploring food with a loving adult is so valuable in encouraging independent thinking, problem-solving, and creativity. There are so many opportunities to show pride in your Little Chef. All they are looking for is an opportunity to make you smile, but they gain so much more on top of that.

Raising Adventurous Eaters

Think of the long-term goal of childhood nutrition: It's not a child who will begrudgingly eat all the broccoli off their plate; it's a child who will joyfully eat and enjoy a variety of flavors. Although a study found that children who help prepare a snack or meal are more likely to try it, that's not the goal in the short term. I always remind parents during Toddler Test Kitchen™ classes, "It's all about the smile, not the bite!"

Sharing space in the kitchen with your Little Chef brings them into what was previously only *your* space. And believe it or not, your child thinks that you are the coolest person alive, and they want to make you happy. By sharing that time and space with them, you help build their confidence and their sense of self-worth. This will lead to confidence at the table when they are faced with the challenge of something new or unfamiliar. The bite of something new and different isn't guaranteed; it's not the measure of success. By joining your child for a fun experience involving food—whether that's food preparation, gardening, or engaging in conversation in the shopping cart—the simple act of sharing a laugh around food is what will help your child achieve that long-term goal of becoming an adventurous eater.

Turning "Yuck!" into "Yum!"

Involving your child in a fun cooking activity can help selective ("picky") tendencies by providing a gentle exposure to ingredients. Even parents who provide a positive environment at the table, who present food in a neutral way, and encourage independence in their children through the use of division of responsibility, may still feel some pushback from their children when it comes to trying new foods. According to the division of responsibility, created by Ellyn Satter, the parent or caregiver is responsible for what is served, where it is served, and when it is served, and the child is responsible for whether they eat and how much they eat. But even when following this perfectly, which takes practice, the table environment itself comes with expectations that may overwhelm hesitant eaters. This is particularly challenging for those children with sensory sensitivities. (More on that on page 135.)

Food is an all-encompassing sensory experience, and that can truly be overwhelming. By cooking with your child, you introduce ingredients in a place that isn't the table and in a way that doesn't ask that they sit still or even nibble anything. When a child cooks, they are free to touch the carrot as they peel, smell the banana as they slice it, and listen to the snap pea do its snapping thing with zero expectation that they will take a bite. That complete lack of expectation allows the child to explore freely. Yes, this may result in the child tasting an ingredient in the process, but they don't feel the pressure to do so. That being said, once you begin to share the cooking experience with your child, you'll quickly learn which ingredients you may need to keep in good stock, because some may not end up in the mixing bowl at all!

Getting a Grasp on Chopping and Mashing

Did you know that your small child can chop? Parents often don't know just how advanced their child's skills are. With the appropriate equipment and the right balance of supervision and independence, a one-year-old can operate a blender, an 18-month-old can mash, and a two-year-old can confidently chop, peel, spread, and roll!

Cooking at a very young age supports both fine and gross motor skills. The palmar grasp is the action of bringing the fingers toward the palm, grasping an object by using the full fist. The pincer grasp, which begins developing at around nine months, is the action of using the pointer finger and thumb to grab an object. (Think about how you might pick up a Cheerio.) The young child working on their pincer grasp skills can practice both palmar and pincer grasping by mashing dough in their little fist. Even the newest Little Chef can start with mixing, spreading, and operating blender buttons to support their developing hand-eye coordination.

As a child grows, reading, math, and science (as food chemistry) can become the focus of kitchen activities. In this way, food-based activities can encourage health, teach a valuable life skill set, and support academic pursuits, all in one!

To maximize the child's benefit, stand back and let your Little Chef take the lead. Step in for safety and to provide assistance when necessary, but allow your child to show off their developing skills. You may be pleasantly surprised to learn what they are capable of!

The Importance of Playtime

This book brings playtime to the kitchen in order to create something fun and educational—something that brings food peace to both you and your Little Chef.

We know that playtime is important for childhood development. One could also argue that playtime remains important throughout childhood and well into adulthood. Laughter decreases anxiety, and for kids, getting a little messy increases comfort. That comfort leads to confidence, which shows up as an adventurous attitude at the table.

It's been proven that young children who are allowed to play with their food are faster to learn food-related vocabulary. Play inspires increased communication. It nurtures imagination, encourages creativity, assists in the development of problem-solving skills, and reduces stress. Ultimately, play provides a context for learning, where the child can develop and acquire all these skills and many more in a real-life way, all while spending essential bonding time with a loving parent, sibling, grandparent, or caregiver.

Getting Started

It's never too early or too late to invite your Little Chef into the kitchen. The infant can be involved from a carrier or bouncy seat. The older child can sit in a highchair and play with a food-based sensory bin containing foods representing different colors, shapes, and textures. Even before a child is ready to eat, they will benefit from exposure to the sights, sounds, and smells that create a warm and loving cooking environment.

LINE COOK: 12 to 24 months

The Line Cook steps in the book are intended for children around 12 to 24 months old. Each child develops at a different pace. Use your own knowledge of your child when determining what will work best, but also be sure to allow your child the independence to develop. Try something that may seem a little bit too advanced. Your toddler will often surprise you with their capability! If it doesn't work out, you can always provide more assistance.

A child at this age will not yet be capable of following instructions, so it's best to give one step at a time and to use a hand-over-hand method when cooking with this Little Chef.

Here's the hand-over-hand ladder of success:

1. **Little Chef's Hand over Adult Hand.** Perform a cooking action with Little Chef's hand over your adult hand.

2. **Adult Hand over Little Chef's Hand.** As Little Chef develops in ability and confidence, switch to Little Chef's hand on the kitchen tool with your adult hand on top.

3. **Little Chef in Charge.** This happens closer to 24 months but may happen as early as 18 months.

These are some good indicators to help you know whether you child is ready to earn their chef's hat:

1. The child can stand independently and confidently. You'll still provide a solid and safe place where your child can stand.

2. The child is confident with their pincer grasp.

3. The child pays attention to speech, responding to "uh-oh" or "no."

4. The child can put objects into or take them out of a container and willingly lets go of objects.

In order to create a happy and safe environment, it's important that you, the adult, feel comfortable and confident. If you feel a high level of anxiety while cooking with your Little Chef, take a step back and try again another time.

SOUS CHEF: 18 to 24 months

The Sous Chef steps will cater to a toddler who is around 18 to 24 months old. This child can perform the steps indicated for the Line Cook as well as working toward developing some more advanced skills and independence. At this age, the child is beginning to push boundaries. By allowing the child some responsibility in the kitchen, you help them begin to develop a sense of independence and confidence that may help ease some of that boundary-pushing tension.

The Sous Chef will be confident with the following skills (in addition to the Line Cook skills), indicating their readiness for these steps:

1. The child can follow one-step verbal commands such as "hand me the spoon" or "push this button."

2. The child copies the actions of the adult.

3. The child shows interest in participating in a kitchen activity.

EXECUTIVE CHEF: 24 to 36 months

The Executive Chef steps will cater to most toddlers ages 24 to 36 months. These recipes are also great for older siblings and friends who want in on the action. At this age, even more so than in the previous age groups, there is a wide variety of developmental ability between one Little Chef and another. Use your own gut instinct, as well as your comfort level, to determine how to proceed. As Little Chef grows, opportunities for independence become even more valuable. Try your best to let Little Chef take the lead, only stepping in when necessary. Parenting is full of "no"—this is a great opportunity to say "yes."

In addition to the skills listed for Line Cook and Sous Chef, the Executive Chef will be confident with the following skills, indicating their readiness for these more complex steps:

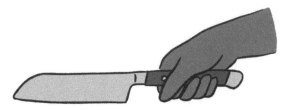

1. The child can understand and follow two-step directions, such as "add the apple to the blender, and then put the lid on the top."

2. The child can make a scribble mark on a piece of paper and turn book pages one at a time.

3. The child can build a tower of four or more blocks.

4. The child displays a desire for independence (which includes acting defiant sometimes).

Playing It Safe

Kitchen activities can be dangerous when age, development, and proper tools and equipment are not taken into account. In this section, I'll give guidance regarding how to create a safe and enjoyable environment for both you and your Little Chef.

Oven-Baked and No-Cook Recipes

The recipes contained in this book are designed to give Little Chef a chance to fully take the lead. For this reason, they will be mostly oven-baked or no-cook. Cooking at the stovetop requires a lot of coordination for both Little Chef and their adult assistant, coordination that either is inappropriate for the child's age or simply may detract from all the fun. When stovetop heat is necessary, such as in the Cheese and Vegetable Quesadilla (page 78) and Chocolate Fruit Tacos (page 128), an electric griddle can provide a stable and safe cooking environment.

To create a safe environment, the proper tools are necessary. Here are some suggestions I have. You can find visuals for these pieces of equipment on my Pinterest board dedicated to the subject (page 135).

TODDLER KNIVES. A great toddler knife is well balanced, has a wide handle for solid gripping, and is sharp enough to cut fruits and veggies but not little fingers. I'm a big fan of Curious Chef products because they are long-lasting and remain appropriate from the littlest of Little Chefs throughout childhood.

CUTTING BOARD. The perfect cutting board will have grips on the bottom to prevent slipping while Little Chef is working. Avoid working with glass, which is louder and brings unnecessary risk. A wooden or plastic cutting board will meet your needs nicely.

LEARNING TOWER. Little Chef needs a secure place to stand. A learning tower provides safety and security. These can be expensive, so check around at consignment shops for the best price or consider a DIY project to create your own learning tower, such as the well-known IKEA BEKVAM stool-to-tower hack (page 135)!

PEELER. A basic peeler is great to have on hand. You don't have to get fancy here; just look for one with a wide-grip handle. It also has to be effective at peeling. If it drives you crazy, it will be a bigger obstacle for Little Chef.

BLENDER OR FOOD PROCESSOR. These are useful for many different recipes. From smoothies to shredded veggies and blender muffins (like the Hulk Muffins, page 91), you'll find yourself using this tool time and again.

SPIRALIZER. If you're into spiralizing (and, really, it's so much fun for Little Chef), you'll want to invest in a spiralizer with a crank. Spiralizers that resemble hourglass peelers are less pricey but are not safe for little fingers. My favorite is the Smile Mom Spiralizer Vegetable Slicer because it has a downward pushing motion that really works well for Little Chef.

Choking Hazards

Choking hazards remain a concern until four years of age. Although cooked food doesn't pose the same risk as when raw, it's important to remember that Little Chef may be tasting throughout the cooking process.

Avoid choking hazards until four years of age, including these foods:

✿ Whole nuts and hard seeds

✿ Hot dogs

✿ Whole grapes, grape tomatoes, cherry tomatoes

✿ Hard, gooey, and sticky candy, including taffy, gum, and marshmallows

✿ Certain raw vegetables and fruits, including carrots and apples

✿ Chunks of nut or seed butter (Note: It is safe to cook with these if Little Chef is simply tasting with a finger dipped in nut or seed butter.)

✿ Chunks of meat or cheese

✿ Raisins and dried cranberries

✿ Fish with bones

✿ Popcorn

Any small, round foods (like grapes or cherry tomatoes) should be halved or quartered to ensure safe tasting. Crisp, raw fruits and vegetables, such as carrots, apples, and jicama, are perfectly safe when spiralized, shredded, or cut into matchsticks.

Allergies and Food Sensitivities

Allergies and food sensitivities are an increasingly common concern. In my book *Stage-by-Stage Baby Food Cookbook*, I discuss how current research supports exposing children to potential allergens early on in the food introduction journey. Current medical advice supports exposing babies to nut butters and other common allergens as some of the first foods offered, at around six months or when baby displays food readiness signs.

If you're joining me on this journey with a Little Chef who has allergy or intolerance obstacles, know that I'll provide alternatives for common allergenic ingredients in order to make cooking safe and fun for everyone. Children often outgrow food allergies by the time they hit teenage years, but this depends largely on the allergen and the type of reaction. Be sure to always discuss safety precautions surrounding food allergens with your pediatrician.

Knife Skills and Equipment Safety

Remember that a toddler knife is still a knife—it's meant to cut, and that means that certain safety precautions must be taken. Many people opt to use a disposable plastic knife for cooking with kids, but I advise against that. Disposable plastic knives have a thin handle that's difficult for Little Chef to grip, and they often break, exposing sharp angles. They also often slip, putting little fingers at risk. This is why it's important to have a child-safe knife ready for Little Chef and all the delicious dishes they will create!

Little Chef may be ready for their chef's knife around 24 months old. This is when some children have developed the focus and combination of fine and gross motor skills to be able to manage the knife safely. If you try it out and it's not working well for Little Chef, simply take a deep breath, put your adult hand over Little Chef's hand, and proceed with the recipe.

Some important considerations for knife safety:

1. **Explain that the knife is a tool, not a toy.** We pick it up to cut, and then we put it back down. The knife stays in the kitchen, and we only touch it when we are cutting something with an adult next to us.

2. **Maintain your cool.** Much like with anything else, an action we perform with joy will become a fun pastime. If the adult is anxious or upset, Little Chef will associate kitchen activities with stress. It's also important to recognize when Little Chef is tired or uninterested—you can always try cooking again another time.

3. **Demonstrate the skill.** Showing Little Chef the action that is expected will allow them to proceed confidently. Different foods may require different cutting actions, such as sawing versus pushing. You may need to display the action a few times.

4. **Use a solid surface.** Little Chef needs a solid surface for both standing and cutting. The step stool should be solid with no rocking. The countertop should hit between Little Chef's waist and chest. The cutting surface should have grips on the bottom to avoid slippage.

5. **Be sure that the food itself is also stable.** This means cutting a banana or zucchini lengthwise in order to provide a solid surface. This will prevent the food from moving back and forth as Little Chef cuts.

6. Begin with softer foods. Advance slowly toward more firm (challenging) foods so that Little Chef has an opportunity to develop confidence in this new and advanced skill.

Certain foods can be prepped ahead of time to account for safety and ability. For example, if you're cutting a melon with a beginner Little Chef, the melon itself can be washed by Little Chef, it can be cut across the middle by the adult assistant, the seeds can be scooped by Little Chef, the melon can be peeled by the adult assistant, and the melon can be cut by Little Chef. This comes with the added bonus of reinforcing patience and the concept of taking turns.

In this book, I also provide recipes that require a blender. Little Chef can add foods to the blender and operate the buttons with supervision. This is a good opportunity to show Little Chef that the bottom of the blender has a sharp blade and that it's dangerous for little fingers.

Demonstrate the safe motion of dropping food into the main compartment of the blender from a distance well above the blades. The oven also comes with some danger. You can explain to Little Chef that the adult must put the food into the oven, but be sure to turn on the oven light so Little Chef can participate in this step from a safe place.

Preparing for Food Play

Food play is an important way for kids to interact with food in a positive and no-pressure way. The Little Chef who is hesitant when it comes to new foods may benefit from simply playing and experiencing the non-bite aspects of unfamiliar food. There are a few things to keep in mind to ensure a fun time for all.

Mind the "Amber Zone"

Your Feeding Team coined a term called the "Amber Zone," which is the idea that even if you think you are positively encouraging your child to eat a food, they might perceive it as negative pressure depending on your intent. Children are very perceptive, and they can pick up on any agenda you might have. Be sure to keep all recipe creation and food-based activities positive and child led. If Little Chef feels like you're trying to get them to touch or eat something they are not comfortable with, if they are anxious around food, or if you have recently made a change from bargaining and bite-counting to a pressure-free meal, take it slowly and be sure to respond to Little Chef's reluctance with compassion and flexibility.

Sensory Processing Difficulties and Food Exploration

Food exposure can be challenging for Little Chefs with sensory processing difficulties. According to Hana Eichele, MOT, OTR/L (see Resources, page 135), food represents all five basic senses: sight, smell, sound, touch, and taste. In addition, there are three sensory systems at work as the body integrates external information with internal feelings, such as movement of body parts. These all work together when exploring and consuming food. This means that food can abruptly overwhelm a sensitive child. Consider these swaps to move slowly when exploring a wide range of foods:

1. **Start with a visual sense.** Allow your child to see food from across the room. Invite them to get closer to it when they are ready.

2. **Work on talking about small smells and BIG smells rather than judgment words, such as *sticky* or *gross*.** Start with cold items that have a smaller smell than some warm foods. You could also place food in a clear container for your child to explore and then briefly open the lid for a smell.

3. **For sticky or slippery foods, offer a utensil or kitchen tool to explore the food rather than requiring them to use their hands.** This can give them time to integrate their visual and smell senses before touching the food.

4. **Adjust recipes to meet the needs of your family by changing the flavor of food.** Just like adults add salt to their meals, kids may want to boost their flavor in a new way. You can add less seasoning to a dish while it's cooking and then, when serving, add more of the seasoning or a dip on the side for those ready to boost flavor. Validate your child's experience to create a safe place where Little Chef can discuss what bothers them about a food experience. Naureen Hunani, RD, suggests this type of dialogue:

Child: *"I don't like the slimy feeling from this plum."*

Parent: *[validate] "That sounds like an uncomfortable feeling." [normalize] "Everyone prefers different flavors or textures." [provide a solution] "You don't have to eat it. Would you like an apple instead?"*

Remember, building a relationship with food takes time. Be the person your child trusts by honoring the speed they are able to explore. In time, they will be a Little Chef who loves the kitchen!

How to Use This Book

If you want to pass on a love of food and food enjoyment to your Little Chef, you're in the right place. I will provide different ways of introducing food beyond the dining room table—from growing and harvesting food to basic food art on the plate—in an effort to explain the gentle food exposure that will help you raise an adventurous eater.

The activities in this book are written for adults to prepare and are meant for all toddler levels. Modifications can be made for supplies or individual developmental or sensory needs. Invite Little Chef to join in the fun activity, being careful to respect their possible reluctance to handle an unfamiliar food. Allow Little Chef to take the lead, and if it's not working out, take it a little more slowly. Modify or take a break and come back to it (or another activity) at another time. Although many activities are linked to recipes, they can be enjoyed either while creating something delicious or at a different time.

The Adult Steps and the three toddler takeover indications—Line Cook, Sous Chef, and Executive Chef—will help you determine which recipe steps should be performed by the adult and which are appropriate cooking actions for Little Chef. If your child is between stages, or you're not quite sure they are ready for the next step, consider allowing them to try more difficult steps as independently as is safe and possible, and watch the smile that accompanies the knowledge that Little Chef can, in fact, do difficult things. That knowledge will benefit them in so many areas of their young lives. If it's not working out, you can always place your hand on top of Little Chef's hand and continue. Create a safe and joyful environment for food exploration that will lead to increased confidence, an adventurous perspective at the table, and a variety of accepted foods that are associated with increased health and food enjoyment.

What is a serving? For recipe standardization reasons, all recipes are provided in adult servings. At the table it's a different story. A child's serving size is the size of their fist, and it grows with them. At any given time, a child may eat a serving size, or they may eat more or less. As long as they are listening to their appetite, the actual amount they consume isn't very important.

Here are some labels and tips you'll find in this book:

✿ **Line Cook, Sous Chef**, and **Executive Chef** labels (pages 5–8) are associated with ages and stages of development. As each child develops at a different rate, consider your Little Chef and how they may benefit most.

✿ The **Toddler Skills Tip** is an indication of skills needed to accomplish an activity with minimal frustration. A small amount of frustration may serve to help the child advance!

✿ The **Safety Tip** serves to provide you with any additional information that may be useful for safety reasons.

✿ **Mix It Up** indicates the possible alterations to an activity to make it slightly more or slightly less challenging. You can use these tips to customize the activity for your own Little Chef.

✿ **Messy Hands** indicates a recipe that is likely to get messy! Messy play is essential during a child's development. It provides Little Chef with a tactile and sensory experience that will inspire their curiosity and allow them to explore the world around them. This serves to enhance their learning, language, and creativity. If your Little Chef is hesitant around mess, you can start with gloves. If your child isn't comfortable with that, try taking over most of the messy steps yourself. At the same time, give a small amount of the messy ingredient(s) to Little Chef in their own bowl, allowing them to decide if, when, and how to interact with the recipe.

✿ Dietary labels include **Dairy-Free, Gluten-Free, Nut-Free, Vegan**, and **Vegetarian**. Please check your product package to ensure that your product has been processed in a certified gluten-free facility.

✿ **Nutrition Tips** are positive and fun facts about the nutrition provided in the recipe.

✿ **Playtime!** indicates fun ways to use ingredients from the recipe to increase your laughter!

Baked Chickpea, Sweet Potato, and Spinach Empanadas

PAGE 70

Start an Eggshell Garden
PAGE 72
▼

CHAPTER TWO

Adventurous Activities

When food becomes familiar and comfortable, kids are more likely to feel confident in trying something new. Many different activities can be a springboard for food familiarization! As you create your meal calendar, select recipes, create your shopping list, and go shopping, consider ways you can include your Little Chef. This chapter will focus on activities that happen away from the kitchen but still focus on food.

Benefits of Food-Focused Activities

Cooking together isn't the only non-meal way to enjoy some happy, food-centric time. In this section, I will present some different activities that can provide food-based conversation and interaction to support the development and refinement of the skills mentioned in chapter 1. The main skill we will work to develop in this section is an adventurous outlook!

Educational Opportunities

The kitchen is the perfect stage for visual and tactile learning of basic math and language skills, skills that will be reinforced in preschool. But you can also rely on a creative shopping list, your home or neighborhood garden, or fun online videos to provide conversation to reinforce colors, counting, shapes, vocabulary, and basic reading skills. There is so much to discuss when it comes to food. By using the activities outlined in this book, you can bring a strong educational aspect to food that will make learning these skills more efficient, fun, and long-lasting.

Understanding the World

Food is the doorway to your own history, and in sharing dishes enjoyed through generations of family, you lovingly pass down your own culture to the next generation. Food is also your passport to the rest of the world. From discussing the origins of a particular food to trying dishes from another place on the globe, the delicious study of food can help you create common ground with those who come from somewhere else. Food can help you discuss cultural, racial, and religious identity, creating an open place in the mind where there is room for compassion and understanding to grow.

Cooking as a Creative Outlet

Being a kid is difficult. Do you remember how all your decisions were made for you? And often without your input?

As children grow and develop, they have a need to exert themselves, to show the world the little seedling personality taking root and starting to grow in a unique way. As a small child picks up a toddler-safe knife and slices a banana, they see how they have taken something from its original form and changed it. As they add pieces of vegetables to a coffee-stirrer skewer, they create a unique and colorful design. Cooking is a fantastic creative outlet for the child who wants to display their own flair.

As the child gets older and begins to understand the function of different ingredients (food chemistry), you can let them take the lead and create a new recipe together. This creative outlet is a wonderful way to support the child's self-esteem and confidence.

Fun with Food Outside the Kitchen

Cooking together introduces food in a setting away from the table. This gives the reluctant eater an opportunity to feel safe when interacting with unfamiliar foods, allowing them to develop confidence around food in general. By bringing this same conversation to the grocery store or the garden, we remove it even more from the table and mealtime, further reducing the pressure to eat. Have fun with these! Remember that laughter can always be your soundtrack.

 ## Grocery Shopping

Grocery shopping can be stressful when you're trying to coax your child into behaving. Instead, try to view the grocery store as a natural classroom, full of possibilities for learning and laughing.

The produce aisle is an amazing resource for conversations about color, shape, number, and how different plants grow. Even if your child isn't communicating verbally yet, they are absorbing all your words and excitement.

Try these conversation starters, or make up your own, finding inspiration in the vibrant aisles:

✿ "These grapes are green, and these are red. They all grow on a vine. These peppers are also red and also grow on a vine, but see how different they look?"

✿ "Should we buy these orange carrots or those multicolored ones? Do you think they taste the same?"

✿ "This green apple is round. Can you find something else that's round?"

✿ "Kiwis are sweet and tart. Can you feel how fuzzy the skin is?"

✿ "Those bananas are a little bit green. That means they are not ready to eat right now. Do you think they will be ready tomorrow?"

Draw out your shopping list and ask the child to help you find the foods you need. If you're not into drawing, capture some pictures online and print out a shopping collage.

Visiting a Vegetable Farm

When looking for a farm to visit, browse the website ahead of time so you know what's in season and available for your picking pleasure. If you live in the city, you might be able to locate a convenient U-Pick location because there has been an increase in urban farming.

When you know what's ripe and ready, you can even look up a few recipes with your Little Chef to get them excited about nature's very own game of hide-and-seek!

On the way to the farm, ask your child what they would like to find. Tell your Little Chef about your favorite way to eat their chosen item, and ask them how they might prepare it. If your child is not yet expressing themselves verbally, just tell them about your own excitement.

Much like in the grocery store, you can easily discuss colors and methods of growth. Ask your Little Chef, "What color is this plant? Is the whole plant the same color?" "This grows on a bush. What else grows on a bush? Let's find out!"

Some other great questions to ask include:

✿ **"How do you think we pick this?"** Explain how some food plants are easy to harvest but others are more complicated. For example, broccoli is cut with a sharp knife along its base, whereas carrots are pulled out of the ground by their "hair." Some plants are better at hide-and-seek than others, and some plants have multiple parts that are edible in different ways—beets, for example.

✿ **"Can you describe the smell?"** and **"What do you think it might taste like?"** Start with the basics, like *sweet* or *tart*, and expand your vocabulary to *earthy* or *delicate*. If you have fun with this, you will automatically convey joy to your Little Chef.

✿ **"How should we prepare this?"** Explain how you can roast the vegetables in the oven, eat them raw, or make a quiche (or "egg pie"). With little ones, this will be a one-sided conversation. When asking bigger kids, be prepared to follow through on their suggestion.

 ## Gardening

If you're ready to take this into new territory after a fun trip to the farm, get your soil and trowel ready. We are starting a garden!

Growing your own food may seem daunting, but there are many ways to start small. As you build up your own confidence and develop your own green thumb, you can start with an herb plant from your local gardening department or grocery store.

If you're ready for the next step, you can get an herb garden kit online and plant seeds together, showing your child that just as they start off small and get bigger, so does the plant.

If you're ready for something a bit more adventurous, play the "Find the Seed" game at the table when eating oranges, peppers, or even watermelon. Put a small cup or bowl in front of Little Chef and have them collect the seeds they find. There are many resources available online and locally to help you germinate, plant, and transfer your seedlings as needed. Your local library might even host a seed exchange where new and experienced gardeners gather to share seeds, stories, and suggestions.

Harvesting with children is amazing, particularly when harvesting something they have been a part of growing. While watering, fertilizing, and even singing to your fledgling vegetable community, discuss with your Little Chef how plants grow and how you know when they are ready to eat. When the time comes, have a harvesting party, plan a recipe, and maybe even get some fun party plates to go with dinner.

Cuisine Around the World

Food is a great way to teach kids about the world. If you have a globe, spin it and play "Geography Roulette," learning about the culture and cuisine of the country you choose. If you have a flat map, play "Pin the Flag on the Country," pinning a mini homemade family flag on a random spot!

You can start easy by focusing on a single ingredient that's common in that area, or you can go full force by making a whole dish or even a whole meal from that distant locale. If you do go for a whole meal, be sure to include something familiar for any reluctant kids (or adults) who may need to just dip their toes in your cuisine adventure.

Once you have your target selected, head over to Google or Pinterest to find common ingredients in the cuisine, including the seasonings used. Use YouTube to find a recipe video and watch it together. There are a few recipes in this very book that will work nicely with this game: Miso Ramen with Mixed Vegetables (page 60), Baked Chickpea, Sweet Potato, and Spinach Empanadas (page 70), and Tabbouleh with Fresh Herbs (page 104).

Discuss how people eat in this country—do they use hands or utensils? Are their utensils the same as ours? How is their food or eating style the same as yours? How is it different? This is a great springboard conversation for discussing how people come from different places and enjoy different flavors, but how we all share the same map!

Reading Books

Reading to young children helps them learn sounds, words, and language, leading to the development of early literacy skills. They learn to value books and stories, which helps stretch their brains and fuels creativity and curiosity. Reading also improves social and communication skills.

Reading books that provide an exciting but pressure-free message about food counts as food exposure. Hesitant eaters need between 15 and 40 exposures to an unfamiliar food in order to feel comfortable interacting with that new item.

Here are some guidelines for what to look for in a book:

1. **Neutral messaging about food.** Many books about food that are directed at kids attempt to send a message of balanced nutrition, but it very often

comes across as black-and-white thinking. Foods are classified into "good" or "bad" or even the tamer "always, sometimes, never" concepts. Although it sounds like a good idea to teach your children about nutrition and about which foods support physical growth, I advise you to steer clear of these messages. Kids are not able to conceptualize moderation. If they hear "cake is bad," they understand "cake is bad, and I'm a bad person for eating it, and Mommy is a bad person for giving it to me."

When the focus is on physical growth, we also miss the cultural implications of the relationship with food. We do celebrate birthdays with cake, and holidays with certain specific dishes. This is an important part of communicating nutrition—understanding how food isn't just for physical growth but for the celebration of culture and connection. When we label foods, we disregard this essential aspect. And the foods we disparage now are the foods Little Chef will seek once we are no longer in charge of their nutrition.

2. **Neutral messaging about body size.** There are many books that create a link between certain foods and body size. People, young and old, come in all different shapes and sizes. In passing these oversimplified links on to our children, kids receive the message that people in larger or smaller bodies are doing something wrong. Body size is much more complex than we have been led to believe, and we can focus on a broader definition of health in more positive ways.

Instead of focusing on body size, we can shift the conversation to focus on healthy habits such as getting enough sleep, eating different kinds of food, and having fun while moving our bodies.

If you're making tacos for dinner, consider reading *Dinosaurs Love Tacos*. If you're going to a food truck event, check out *Food Trucks!* And if you're starting that herb garden we spoke about, be sure to read *Growing Vegetable Soup*. For more reading suggestions, head over to my Pinterest board "Books and Gadgets." You can find the link in the Resources section on page 134.

 ## Watching Shows About Food

The sheer number of resources at our fingertips is amazing. And that's a knife that can cut both ways. When using YouTube as a platform to spur food-based learning or conversation, you want to watch out for the same pitfalls mentioned in the Reading Books section. There are many cartoons and cartoon-like personalities trying to get out a positive food message but missing the mark.

When searching YouTube, be specific, typing in things like:

- ✿ "How do pineapples grow, for kids?"

- ✿ "Goldfish eating broccoli"

- ✿ "Where does pizza come from?"

- ✿ "Hamster eating burrito"

Then be sure to screen for content and messaging. Make sure the video is age-appropriate and doesn't contain any unnecessary advice regarding the health status of the food item, how often it should be consumed, or messages about body size.

Time the video with the unfamiliar dish that will soon appear on the table. If you're serving a delicious Ethiopian lentil stew, consider finding a video about how lentils grow and a second video about how people in Ethiopia eat with their hands and with a special sourdough flatbread called *injera*.

If you're serving hamburgers, consider finding a fun video about the invention of hamburgers and how people eat them in different places.

You can always find fun animals eating pretty much anything you're planning to serve. Couple one of those fun videos with an imitation of that animal at the table!

Coloring and Other Art

Food art doesn't have to be complex and Pinterest-worthy. Making a simple smiley face with a banana and a couple of strawberries could put a smile on your Little Chef's face. Have them join in the fun by asking your little one to make a silly face and then trying to capture their precious expression with whatever you have on hand.

Coloring is a super fun way to engage kids in pressure-free food interaction. For the youngest kids, a color- or shape-matching game would be appropriate. As the child gets older, coloring sheets, like the ones found in *Let's Play with Our Food: My Fruit and Veggie Coloring Book* by Arielle Dani Lebovitz and Mary Navarro, generate creative and gentle food exposure.

To bring it a step closer to the dinner table, use food to create painting stamps. By using potatoes, carrots, beets, celery, and radishes, you can create fun shapes that are great for painting. Avoid fruit in this activity because the higher moisture content might cause the paint to thin out too much.

You can also create a beautiful paint palette by using spices. Turmeric, nutmeg, paprika, cinnamon, cumin, cardamom, and cocoa can be mixed with a few drops of water and then used with your veggie stamps to create a beautiful and tasty work of art!

If your child seems very interested in using spices, kick that up a notch with some fun homemade herb and spice play dough (page 84).

 ## Food Games

Games are key to encouraging curiosity and fostering an adventurous outlook. Here are a few to try:

SINK OR FLOAT

Inspired by Arielle Dani Lebovitz, RD, this game introduces early physics concepts. When serving a new fruit or vegetable (because meat and dairy, generally, don't work so well with this one), ask your Little Chef, "Do you think this will sink or float?" Set up a pitcher with water and test it out. Try it with whole fruits or veggies and then again after they are cut—is there a difference in the result?

FRUITY SKEE-BALL

This new twist on a classic game is credited to Arielle Dani Lebovitz, RD. It can get a little competitive if you want it to be!

You'll need:

- A cardboard box and markers to make the scoreboard

- Watermelon rind halves or quarters

- Ping pong balls or similar

Using a marker, draw three circles, one on top of the next. The lowest circle is worth 10 points, the middle 40 points, and the top circle 50 points. Draw a circle on either side of the 50-point circle and assign them each 100 points.

Place your rind halves or quarters in each circle, stand back a few feet, and toss the ball into the rinds! How many balls can you get in the rind?

You can use other melon rinds, a hollowed-out pumpkin or other squash, or Dani's original concept, mango skins.

GUESSING GAMES

In this game, everyone guesses where a food item came from. Did it grow on a tree? On a vine? In a patch? Where in the world did it grow? How did it get to your table? With an older child, you can start to spin stories about magic compost, pirates, and flying carpets. It's all about the laugh!

MEMORY GAMES

Memory card games can be a lot of fun, from the small child enjoying the vibrant colors to the older child who is capable of following the rules. You can purchase or create flash cards with pictures of food and then use those to spur fun food conversation. Ask your child if their favorite food is pictured, if there is a food they are interested in trying, and which food they think is the most colorful. Ask your Little Chef if they can pretend to be that food by making their body into a similar shape. Use a bigger version of the image and ask your child to add stickers or use crayons to draw on a face.

 ## Meal Planning

Meal planning is a great way to involve kids in their own nutrition. At the table, I recommend the division of responsibility. The parent decides what is served, where it is served, and when it is served. The child determines whether they will eat and how much they will eat. Keep these roles clear. Avoid allowing the child to take over the adult's job by providing a special kid-food meal, but refrain from infringing on the child's responsibilities by counting bites or bargaining.

Allowing the child to help with meal planning can go wrong if it isn't done in a way that accounts for the child's age and stage of development. Children ages 12 to 24 months do not yet understand the concept of planning. When they are being asked for input, it must be input for a meal that is happening in the next 5 to 10 minutes. Provide the child with no more than two choices: "Would you like carrots or cucumbers with lunch?"

When creating a plate with your Little Chef, you can ask, "How many colors are on this plate? Do you think we are missing anything? How can we create a rainbow?" But the child may say that you're missing brown and that some chocolate pudding might rectify the problem. Consider agreeing; enjoying food together means enjoying all kinds of food—bananas and chocolate pudding alike (and sometimes together!).

As the child grows and develops, they can take a more meaningful role. The 4-year-old can help select a side dish to go with a meal for later that day, or perhaps breakfast the next morning. They also may be able to choose between three to four options.

By the time the child is 6 or 7 and has been a Little Chef for a while, they may actually be able to help create the weekly meal plan, determine part of the shopping list, and even prepare snacks or lunches with minimal help—doesn't that sound exciting?

 ## General Food Play

An adventurous attitude around food comes from a combination of confidence and laughter. Some simple food play can provide both. Here are some fun ideas for you:

JEWELRY MAKING. Can you make a bracelet or ring with a snack?

EDIBLE SANDBOX. Blend up some Cheerios and use the edible "sand" you've created as a fun-filled sensory snack. Hide some edible treasure in the sandbox, being sure to steer clear of any choking hazards.

MELON BALL SENSORY PLAY. Start off with a fun melon guessing game. Buy a new melon and guess what it looks like on the inside! Have your Little Chef help you scoop out the seeds and make some melon balls. Pretend they are eyeballs! Roll them around, make a face out of them, or just reach into a bowl of melon balls and talk about what it feels like.

YOGURT PAINTING. Set your table with pancakes, tortillas, or a different flatbread and some yogurt. Using little fingers, paint on the bread with the yogurt. Make a rainbow, a smiley face, or the Batman symbol. Get creative!

The goal of food play is laughter. Laughter counteracts anxiety and encourages confidence. This, along with the added bonus of sharing a fun activity with a loved one, helps create new neural pathways, helping the child begin to see food as safe and, even more importantly, as fun.

Banana
Sushi

PAGE 36
▼

▲

Cut Banana Peels into a Squid
PAGE 38

CHAPTER THREE

Morning Games at Breakfast

Sensational Berry Smoothie

MAKES 6 (4-OUNCE) SERVINGS · **PREP TIME:** 5 MINUTES

Smoothies are refreshing and delicious and can be packed with nutrition! Little Chef can work on gross motor skills and hand-eye coordination by adding ingredients to the blender. This recipe includes a quarter avocado to support brain development, but fat also helps older kids and adults with mood regulation.

DAIRY-FREE OPTIONAL, GLUTEN-FREE, NUT-FREE, VEGAN OPTIONAL, VEGETARIAN

½ cup yogurt, kefir, or a non-dairy alternative
1 medium banana, fresh or frozen
¼ avocado
1 cup frozen or fresh raspberries, strawberries, blackberries, or a mix
1½ cups packed spinach

1. **ADULT STEP** Set up the blender, showing Little Chef the blades and explaining that they are dangerous. See page 32 for an activity that directly relates to this that can be done before this recipe or while the blender does its work.

2. **LINE COOK** Put the yogurt in the blender.

3. **LINE COOK** Add the banana, avocado, berries, and spinach to the blender.

4. LINE COOK Blend until smooth or until desired consistency is reached. For a thinner smoothie, add a splash of milk or milk alternative until desired texture is reached.

5. ADULT STEP Pour into cups with lids and straws.

✪**TODDLER SKILLS TIP:** The intense sound of the blender helps acclimate your little one to louder noises. If your child has trouble with loud noises, ask them to add ingredients to the blender; then you can turn it on as they watch from afar. You can make a game of moving closer and closer to the blender, but be careful to avoid pushing Little Chef completely out of their comfort zone.

✪**NUTRITION TIP:** I rarely recommend including protein powder in food meant for Little Chef. We often overestimate the amount of protein kids need. If added protein is needed, as determined with your doctor or dietitian, consider adding a quarter block of soft tofu to your smoothie.

Pretend to Be a Blender!

With this activity, your child can become familiar with the blender, in both parts and sounds. Pretend play helps build your child's development in language, thinking, and social and emotional areas. As your child discovers the power of imagination, they will find more opportunities to play!

Blender

1. Start by showing Little Chef the parts of the blender, pointing out the blades and explaining that they are dangerous. For the littlest chef, you'll point at the blades and say "ouch!" For more advanced chefs, you can use more language to explain the danger.

2. Practice the sound the blender makes. Is it high pitched or a low growl? Is there a knob where you can turn up the volume?

⭐ **MIX IT UP:** Keep it simple by spinning and making a lot of noise to mimic a blender, or get into it with some energetic music and green construction-paper spinach! Be sure to join Little Chef in this fun adventure for maximum enjoyment and bonding.

Morning Glory Muffins

MAKES 12 MUFFINS • **PREP TIME:** 15 MINUTES • **COOK TIME:** 25 TO 28 MINUTES

Muffins are a staple in my home. They are a great way to pack in nutrition, they freeze well, and they travel well. They are perfect as gentle nutrition exposure for Little Chef, and they are a welcome addition to any breakfast or snack, at home or on the go. Note that this is a thick dough, but the carrots and apples will release moisture as they bake. Because many people wake up ready to eat breakfast, and these take a while until they're ready to eat, be sure to serve a good snack first, or use the recipe for your morning snack, post-breakfast.

••••••••••••••••••••••••••••••••

DAIRY-FREE, GLUTEN-FREE OPTIONAL, MESSY HANDS, NUT-FREE, VEGAN OPTIONAL, VEGETARIAN

½ cup melted coconut oil, butter, or avocado oil, plus more for coating the muffin tin (optional)

1½ cups whole-wheat flour or gluten-free flour

½ cup all-purpose or gluten-free flour

1 tablespoon baking powder

2 teaspoons baking soda

2 teaspoons cinnamon

½ teaspoon salt

¾ cup applesauce

10 Medjool dates, pitted, soaked, and pureed

1 apple, grated

1 tablespoon vanilla extract

2 cups carrot, cleaned and grated

½ cup raisins

••••••••••••••••••••••••••••••••

1. **ADULT STEP:** Preheat the oven to 375°F.

2. **EXECUTIVE CHEF:** Prepare a 12-cup muffin tin with parchment or silicone liners or coat the muffin tin with oil.

3. **LINE COOK:** In a large bowl, combine the whole-wheat flour, all-purpose flour, baking powder, baking soda, cinnamon, and salt.

CONTINUED →

Morning Glory Muffins CONTINUED

4. **LINE COOK:** In a medium bowl, combine the applesauce, dates, oil, apple, and vanilla.

5. **LINE COOK** (with some assistance): Pour the wet ingredients into the dry ingredients and mix until just combined.

6. **LINE COOK:** Fold in the carrot and raisins and mix until just combined.

7. **EXECUTIVE CHEF:** Fill each muffin cup two-thirds full.

8. **ADULT STEP:** Bake for 25 to 28 minutes, until golden and a toothpick inserted comes out clean. Allow muffins to cool on the counter or on a cooling rack.

✪ **TODDLER SKILLS TIP:** If you're using a food processor to shred the apples and carrots, allow your child to put the apple or carrot into the top of the processor. Show them how the blade shreds the food. If you're grating apples and carrots by hand, be sure to leave that to adult hands.

✪ **PLAYTIME!** See if you can use a shredded piece of apple or carrot to make a ring!

Muffin Coloring

Draw or color in a muffin outline while your Morning Glory Muffins bake! Are there carrot eyebrows? A raisin smile? Maybe an apple hat? Can you turn a muffin liner into a smiling sun in a bright blue sky? Coloring is a wonderful, relaxing way to share some creative time together as Little Chef works on their finger grip while practicing focus. It's also a fantastic activity to get Little Chef comfortable around new food.

• •

Muffin liners
Paper
Crayons
GlitterStickers

1. Draw a muffin outline and give the child crayons, or get a little fancier with eyeball stickers and glitter. Increase the fun further by joining your child to make your own art.

⭐ **TODDLER SKILLS TIP:**
If you're using paper and crayons, consider taping the paper to the table to prevent it from moving as Little Chef is coloring. Think about getting some thicker crayons, easier for little hands to grab and use. This is a great sidewalk art activity, too! Use thick pieces of chalk for little hands.

Banana Sushi

MAKES 1 SUSHI ROLL • **PREP TIME:** 10 MINUTES, PLUS OPTIONAL CHILLING TIME

Bananas are the ultimate food. They are tasty and easy to eat. Plus, they pair well with both sweet and savory flavors. This fun twist on traditional sushi provides a wonderful starting point for conversations about size, color, shape, flavor, texture, and more.

....

DAIRY-FREE, GLUTEN-FREE, MESSY HANDS, NUT-FREE OPTIONAL, VEGAN OPTIONAL, VEGETARIAN

1 banana
2 to 3 tablespoons topping mix:

 2 tablespoons nut or seed butter and 2 tablespoons shredded coconut

 2 tablespoons nut or seed butter and 2 tablespoons puffed rice cereal

 2 tablespoons melted dark chocolate and 1 tablespoon chia seeds

 2 tablespoons plain Greek yogurt and 2 tablespoons crushed freeze-dried berries

 2 tablespoons nut or seed butter and 1 medium-sized flour tortilla

....

1. **ADULT STEP:** Pinch off the top of the banana and allow the child to finish peeling it. You can simplify this further for very little hands by superficially slicing the peel lengthwise, leaving a seam where the peel will naturally split.

2. LINE COOK: Roll the banana in the liquid or sticky ingredient of your choice. Depending on your selection, spreading may go a bit more smoothly. Cover the banana as completely as possible.

3. LINE COOK: If you have selected the yogurt, place it in the freezer for 20 to 30 minutes to harden just a bit but still retains some stickiness.

4. SOUS CHEF: Roll the banana in the dry ingredient of your choice, covering as much of the banana as possible. If you are using a tortilla, wrap it around the banana.

5. EXECUTIVE CHEF: Cut the banana into rolls. This may require additional adult help to stabilize the banana so it doesn't roll around.

✪ TODDLER SKILLS TIP: If a child is working on the pincer grasp or just doesn't want to risk messy hands, they can sprinkle toppings onto the banana.

✪ PLAYTIME! Insert a popsicle stick into the bottom of each piece to make lollipops!

Cut Banana Peels into a Squid

Bananas present many opportunities for fun. But what is more fun than a squiggly squid? In this simple activity, we take the banana peels from our banana sushi and give them a life all their own. What will your banana squid eat? Does she like to dance? Can you create a banana squid dance party?

Banana peel
Knife
Good music
Googly eyes
Marker

1. Lay your empty banana peel down and use a knife to cut slits lengthwise, creating tentacles.

2. Add eyes with a marker or by gluing googly eyes to the top near the head of the peel. See if your banana squid would like to eat a piece of banana sushi!

3. Ask your banana squid questions:

   ✿ Where do bananas come from? Where do squids come from?

   ✿ What is the banana squid's name?

   ✿ What does a banana squid like to eat?

✪ **TODDLER SKILLS TIP:** If Little Chef is at the Executive Chef level, they can cut slits for tentacles. Otherwise, Little Chef can draw on eyes or glue on googly eyes!

Do-It-Yourself Oatmeal Bar

SERVES 2 • **PREP TIME:** 10 MINUTES

Serving breakfast, lunch, or dinner in a DIY style allows for minimal prep, minimal waste, and maximum joy! Think about what else you can serve in a deconstructed fashion—tacos, salad, soup, potato bar, and so much more. By serving each ingredient separately, you allow Little Chef to get familiar with some new items on the table on their own terms. When choosing different toppings to set out, include different colors, flavors, and textures. Consider using this meal to stimulate a conversation about each individual option. Use your favorite oats, following the cooking directions on the packaging.

•••••••••••••••••••••••••••••••••••

DAIRY-FREE OPTIONAL, GLUTEN-FREE, MESSY HANDS, NUT-FREE OPTIONAL, VEGAN OPTIONAL, VEGETARIAN

1 cup dry old-fashioned oats

1¾ cups water, milk, or milk alternative

Pinch salt (optional)

Topping options: nut or seed butter, dark chocolate shavings, shredded coconut, toasted sunflower or sesame seeds, granola, chia seeds, plain Greek yogurt, fresh or frozen berries, ground flax meal, chopped nuts, milk or milk alternative, or cinnamon

•••••••••••••••••••••••••••••••••••

1. **ADULT STEP:** Make the oatmeal according to directions on the box. Consider reducing the liquid by a half cup if you're short on time; use milk or milk alternative to cool the oatmeal for Little Chef.

2. **ADULT STEP:** Set out a divided party plate, an ice cube tray, or a few bowls with your chosen toppings. Amounts will vary depending on how many you choose. Include tongs or spoons or let your Little Chef use their fingers.

CONTINUED →

Do-It-Yourself Oatmeal Bar CONTINUED

3. **LINE COOK:** Each person creates their own unique breakfast!

✪ **TODDLER SKILLS TIP:** When choosing serving utensils, consider your Little Chef's developmental phase. What is most likely to cause the least amount of frustration but still challenging your little one appropriately? If your child comes to the table hungry, save the challenge for later in the day. You could also present a few different options for serving—one spoon, one set of tongs, and maybe some training chopsticks with helpers attached for the Executive Chef.

✪ **NUTRITION TIP:** When you sit down to enjoy this mealtime activity along with Little Chef, they are more likely to try a new topping. Consider giving your little one a small plate next to their bowl where they can try something new without adding it to their bowl.

Oatmeal Squish Bowl and Facials!

Use up leftover oatmeal while experiencing the fun texture the meal provides—and hydrating your face in the meantime! This is a messy one, so lay down some towels or move it to the empty bathtub or even the backyard. Experiencing different types of touch and texture helps toddlers develop and strengthen motor skills, and helps build new neural connections in the brain and stimulates language skills.

Prepared oatmeal
Large bowl
Towels

1. Have Little Chef place the cooked oatmeal in a big bowl and squish it between their fingers. You, the adult, should be sure to join in—this is a great stress buster! Watch how the oatmeal squishes out between their fingers. See if Little Chef can make an oatmeal worm!

2. Take it to the next level with an oatmeal facial. Start by putting some oatmeal on your own face and showing your little one how much fun it can be. Your child may want to "assist" you. If Little Chef is into it, have them add some squishy oatmeal to their own face. Make silly faces and be sure to take a few selfies in the process.

CONTINUED →

Oatmeal Squish Bowl and Facials! CONTINUED

✪ **TODDLER SKILLS TIP:** It's very important to make sure that Little Chef is comfortable with any food activity, including both meals and non-meal food play. If your child seems tired or uninterested, or is actively avoiding participation, change tack and do something else. Pursuing an activity that is distasteful to your child may backfire.

✪ **MIX IT UP:** If Little Chef doesn't want to decorate their own face with oatmeal, try blowing up a balloon, drawing on a face, and giving Mr. Balloon an oatmeal facial. Chances are your own face will be the preferred toy in this activity.

Pumpkin Oatmeal Breakfast Cookies

MAKES 16 COOKIES · **PREP TIME:** 15 MINUTES · **COOK TIME:** 15 MINUTES

Who doesn't love a good cookie? Jump on the breakfast-cookie train with this delicious pumpkin spice recipe, perfect for cooking with kids. You can use either canned or homemade pumpkin puree. The baking time is dependent on the water content of your pumpkin, so you may need to bake a few minutes longer when using fresh puree.

••••••••••••••••••••••••••••••••

DAIRY-FREE, GLUTEN-FREE, MESSY HANDS, NUT-FREE, VEGAN OPTIONAL, VEGETARIAN

Olive oil (optional), **to coat the baking sheet**

2 cups old-fashioned oats (not instant)

1 cup pumpkin puree

¼ cup honey or maple syrup

¼ cup flax meal

½ cup sunflower seeds

½ cup dried cranberries

2 teaspoons pumpkin spice

Pinch kosher salt

••••••••••••••••••••••••••••••••

1. **ADULT STEP:** Preheat the oven to 350°F.

2. **EXECUTIVE CHEF:** Prepare a baking sheet by lining it with a sheet of parchment paper or lightly coating with olive oil.

3. **LINE COOK:** In a small bowl, stir all ingredients together until well mixed.

4. **EXECUTIVE CHEF:** Using a quarter-cup measuring scoop, place cookie dough on the prepared baking sheet, leaving about 2 inches between them.

CONTINUED →

Pumpkin Oatmeal Breakfast Cookies CONTINUED

5. **ADULT STEP:** Bake the cookies for 10 to 12 minutes; then turn off the heat, and leave cookies in the oven for another 10 to 12 minutes.

6. **ADULT STEP:** Let the cookies cool outside the oven on the baking sheet and enjoy!

✪ **TODDLER SKILLS TIP:** If your child is scooping cookie dough onto the prepared baking sheet, cookies will likely be different sizes. Just go with that! Your child will recognize the cookies that they made and will be so proud of their super tiny or huge cookie! If there is a lot of variation in cookie sizes, remove the smaller ones when they are done baking and allow the larger cookies to bake longer.

✪ **NUTRITION TIP:** This is a fantastic recipe for kids who are battling constipation. The mix of soluble and insoluble fiber can be very helpful in moving things along. To round this out and make it a meal, serve yogurt on the side or for dipping.

Tasty Painter's Palette

Expand your palate with a flavorful painter's palette of ingredients! Often, children are hesitant when it comes to trying a mixed dish. By separating out the ingredients, you give them an opportunity to get comfortable with each ingredient on its own. This is also a great tool when you're serving a casserole or other mixed dish at dinnertime. Note that dried cranberries were left out of this activity since they are considered a choking hazard until age four. They are not a concern inside the cookies since baking changes the size, shape, and texture.

2 tablespoons old-fashioned oats
1 tablespoon pumpkin puree
1 tablespoon honey
(or maple syrup)
½ tablespoon flax meal
1 tablespoon sunflower seeds
¼ teaspoon pumpkin spice
Pinch kosher salt
Ice cube tray, plates, or bowls

1. Separate out the individual ingredients in the Pumpkin Oatmeal Breakfast Cookie recipe, and put a bit of each ingredient on a plate, in a few bowls, or in an empty ice cube tray.

2. Discuss each ingredient with Little Chef:

   ❁ How does it feel in your hand?

   ❁ Can you squish it between your fingers?

   ❁ What color is it? Can you arrange the ingredients by color?

   ❁ How big is it? Can you organize the ingredients by size?

   ❁ How does it smell?

CONTINUED →

Tasty Painter's Palette CONTINUED

✿ How do you think it tastes?

✿ Do you think it would be loud if you bit into it?

✿ Can you pretend to be an ingredient? Which one?

3. If your little one is older, consider adding in some theoretical questions:

✿ If this ingredient could speak, what would it say?

✿ How would this ingredient walk across the table? Would it roll? Jump? Dance?

✿ What kind of flavor is this ingredient? Which other ingredients are the same type of flavor?

✿ Which two or three ingredients would you pair together for the perfect bite?

✪ TODDLER SKILLS TIP: Kids are naturally curious, and they may express that curiosity by eating their whole flavor plate. That's okay! Prepare two plates: one for tasting and one for discussion. You may end up asking your child questions as they eat their entire plate! It's okay to make this into a one-sided conversation with Little Chef. Allow them to explore!

Spinach
Ribbon
Salad

PAGE 57

CHAPTER FOUR

Fun with Lunch and Dinner

Ribbon Dancing
PAGE 59
▼

Roasted Parmesan Spaghetti Squash

SERVES 8 • **PREP TIME:** 15 MINUTES, PLUS 20 MINUTES TO COOL
BAKE TIME: 40 MINUTES

Spaghetti squash is packed full of nutrition and full of fun. See the process through Little Chef's eyes; join your child in appreciating the wonder and the joy. To add some protein and make this a whole meal, add one can of rinsed black beans.

DAIRY-FREE OPTIONAL, GLUTEN-FREE, MESSY HANDS, NUT-FREE, VEGAN OPTIONAL, VEGETARIAN

1 tablespoon olive oil, plus more to coat the baking sheet

1 medium spaghetti squash, halved lengthwise

2 teaspoons cumin

2 teaspoons garlic powder

1 tablespoon Parmesan cheese

1. **ADULT STEP:** Preheat the oven to 400°F.

2. **EXECUTIVE CHEF:** Prepare a baking sheet by lining it with a sheet of aluminum foil and lightly coating it with olive oil.

3. **EXECUTIVE CHEF:** Rub the olive oil over the flesh side of both halves of the squash and place on the oiled baking sheet, cut-side down.

4. **ADULT STEP:** Bake for about 40 minutes, until fully cooked and soft; then let it cool.

5. **SOUS CHEF:** Remove the seeds and strings.

6. **LINE COOK:** Using two forks, shred the spaghetti squash to make noodles. Place in a large bowl.

7. **LINE COOK:** Sprinkle in the cumin, garlic powder, and Parmesan cheese, and mix well.

✪**TODDLER SKILLS TIP:** Watch your child's face as they create spaghetti strings from squash! Even the youngest of hands can appreciate this fun, sensory activity.

✪**PLAYTIME!** Be sure to allow time and space for fully experiencing the fun that is spaghetti squash! This is a messy hands activity, which is so important for children learning how to interact with food in a positive way. And that often means play!

Spaghetti Squash Happy Face

Messy play is an essential part of childhood. As Little Chef feels the spaghetti squash strands between their fingers, use the opportunity to discuss fun, food-focused vocabulary, like *squishy*, *smooth*, and *stringy*. Messy play allows for the development of creativity and adventurous experimentation. Connecting food with different facial expressions, such as happy, sad, or surprised, reinforces the connection between the face and associated emotions. That creative outlet can help calm strong emotions in both children and adults.

½ cup cooked and shredded spaghetti squash

Handful cooked black beans, either fresh or canned, rinsed

Plate

1. Set out the spaghetti squash and black beans.

2. Make a happy face, a sad face, a laughing face, and a surprised face.

✪ **TODDLER SKILLS TIP:** Depending on the age, mood, or development of your Little Chef, this activity can go in a different direction entirely. That's okay. Whatever kind of interaction your child initiates with these ingredients will be a positive step, as long as you allow them to take the lead. Maybe happy face spaghetti squash isn't in the cards today, but a spaghetti squash rainbow is.

Colorful Salad Bar

SERVES 3 · **PREP TIME:** 10 TO 15 MINUTES

Fruits and vegetables are naturally colorful and perfect for a beautiful salad. Toss all the ingredients together or keep each different item in its own place, allowing each family member to construct their own perfect salad. Create a berry and melon fruit salad or a "veggie-ful" crunch bowl. Use the bright colors to discuss other items around your house: "Does this red pepper remind you of that floral painting?" or "Does this piece of jicama look like a LEGO?" Some cucumbers can be eaten with the peel on, but others have a tough and bitter skin. Wash your cucumber well; then taste a slice with the peel to decide whether it should stay on or go in the compost heap. Ask Little Chef for their opinion, too!

DAIRY-FREE OPTIONAL, GLUTEN-FREE, NUT-FREE, VEGAN OPTIONAL, VEGETARIAN

½ head romaine or other lettuce
1 cucumber
2 carrots
2 celery stalks
1 large tomato
¼ large jicama
2 tablespoons toasted sunflower seeds
Store-bought dressing of choice, **Apple Cider Vinaigrette** (page 55), or **Italian-Style Dressing** (page 55)

1. **LINE COOK:** Wash and dry the lettuce using a salad spinner or let the lettuce dry on a paper towel.

2. **EXECUTIVE CHEF:** Tear the lettuce into small pieces and place in a bowl.

3. **EXECUTIVE CHEF:** Peel the cucumber (if needed).

4. **ADULT STEP:** Slice the cucumber lengthwise to create a flat surface.

5. **EXECUTIVE CHEF:** Slice or chop the cucumber.

CONTINUED →

Colorful Salad Bar CONTINUED

6. **SOUS CHEF** (with some adult help): Peel the carrot into ribbons or shred it in a food processor. Peel the skin off the jicama.

7. **LINE COOK:** Wash the celery.

8. **EXECUTIVE CHEF:** Chop or slice the celery.

9. **ADULT STEP:** Cut the tomato in half.

10. **EXECUTIVE CHEF:** Cut the tomato into slices or chunks and cut the jicama into thick slices.

11. **EXECUTIVE CHEF:** Add all the ingredients to a big bowl and toss or place each ingredient in separate small bowls and serve.

12. **LINE COOK:** Sprinkle the toasted sunflower seeds on top of the salad.

13. **EXECUTIVE CHEF:** Measure out ⅓ cup of the dressing.

14. **LINE COOK:** Add the dressing and toss.

✪ **TODDLER SKILLS TIP:** This is going to be a beautiful, chunky salad. In order to make the most of this recipe, allow your Little Chef to create tiny pieces and pieces larger than you might have cut yourself. Look for reasons to praise your child for this new skill.

✪ **NUTRITION TIP:** It's important for food to both look and taste delicious. Include a tasty dressing for Little Chef to add to their salad if they like. The fat found in many dressings helps the body absorb micronutrients, such as vitamins A, D, E, and K. Fat also supports brain growth in children and mood management in adults. Find a dressing you love and enjoy it.

Flavorful Salad Dressings

Salad dressings add flavor and texture to colorful veggie-based meals, but they are also important for nutrition. These homemade dressings are wonderful with Spiral Squash (page 102) or Colorful Salad Bar (page 53), or simply served as a dip with crunchy veggies!

Apple Cider Vinaigrette

MAKES 1 CUP • **PREP TIME:** 5 MINUTES

½ cup apple cider vinegar

½ cup olive oil

1 tablespoon honey

Pinch salt

Pinch freshly ground black pepper

Pinch dried oregano

1 garlic clove, minced

EXECUTIVE CHEF: Add all ingredients to a small, lidded container and shake until incorporated.

Italian-Style Dressing

MAKES 1 CUP • **PREP TIME:** 5 MINUTES

½ cup olive oil

¼ cup red or white wine vinegar

2 tablespoons water

3 tablespoons Parmesan cheese, grated (or nutritional yeast)

¾ teaspoon dried basil

Pinch dried oregano

¾ teaspoon dried parsley

2 teaspoons honey

1 teaspoon lemon juice

Pinch freshly ground black pepper

¼ teaspoon fresh or frozen garlic, diced

¼ teaspoon salt

Pinch red pepper flakes (optional)

EXECUTIVE CHEF: Add all ingredients to a small, lidded container and shake until incorporated.

Boat Race with Romaine

Using lettuce to make a boat race in the bath reinforces how fun food can be. By including a favorite toy, we further associate food with fun, relaxation, and laughter. This super fun activity is credited to Arielle Dani Lebovitz, RD.

Few pieces of Romaine, or another boat-shaped leaf

Very small toy person, medium pom-pom, or toy of similar size and shape

1. Run a bubble-free bath.

2. From either inside the bath or the side of the bathtub, put the toy inside the lettuce boat and race it to the other end of the bathtub.

✪ **SAFETY TIP:** Be sure to use a toy that is not a choking hazard for your child, given their size and development.

✪ **MIX IT UP:** If you have a slide or pool in the backyard, try this outside!

Spinach Ribbon Salad

SERVES 5 • **PREP TIME:** 30 MINUTES • **COOK TIME:** 15 MINUTES

This recipe uses couscous, a tiny pasta common in Northern Africa and Middle East. Israeli couscous, also called pearl couscous, is a larger granule than other types of couscous you may find. In my house, we call it baby pasta! Couscous can be served hot or cold, sweet or savory. In this recipe, we create a delicious rainbow by adding veggies and a simple and tangy lemon dressing. Here is my special trick for cutting onions: Put on swimming goggles! This works for kids and adults, and it has never let me down once. Just be sure to put them on before the first cut.

DAIRY-FREE, GLUTEN-FREE OPTIONAL, NUT-FREE, VEGAN, VEGETARIAN

1 cup dry Israeli (pearl) couscous

2 tablespoons olive oil, divided

1 cucumber

1 generous handful cherry tomatoes

¼ red onion

2 generous handfuls fresh spinach

1 to 2 tablespoons fresh parsley

1 lemon, cut in half

Kosher salt

1. **ADULT STEP:** Cook the couscous according to package instructions, adding 1 tablespoon of olive oil to the water to prevent clumping. Set aside to cool for about 20 minutes.

2. **EXECUTIVE CHEF:** Peel the cucumber if needed.

3. **ADULT STEP:** Cut the cucumber, tomatoes, and onion in half lengthwise to create a solid surface for cutting.

4. **EXECUTIVE CHEF:** Chop the cucumber, tomatoes, and onion into small pieces.

CONTINUED →

Spinach Ribbon Salad CONTINUED

5. **EXECUTIVE CHEF** (with adult demonstration or assistance): Cut the spinach into ribbons by bunching leaves and rolling them up to form a horizontal line (like a spinach torpedo) and then slicing downward every few centimeters.

6. **EXECUTIVE CHEF:** Chop the parsley by collecting the leaves into a ball and then chopping through the ball until the parsley is the desired size.

7. **LINE COOK:** Mix the cooled couscous with all other ingredients.

8. **SOUS CHEF:** Squeeze the lemon on top, keeping it away from little eyes. You can bring back the goggles for this step for both fun and function.

9. **LINE COOK:** Drizzle on the remaining olive oil, sprinkle a pinch of salt, stir, and enjoy!

✪ **TODDLER SKILLS TIP:** The method of cutting the spinach into ribbons is called *chiffonade*. Practice pronunciation of this French word with Little Chef and consider watching a video together explaining how to chiffonade. Little Chef will love copying the video.

✪ **PLAYTIME!** Boost the fun factor by using your spinach ribbons to make eyebrows or a mustache! Take some fun pictures or videos to laugh about later.

Ribbon Dancing

Children are so intuitive with their bodies. This leads to the kind of fun, joyful dancing that adults are often too self-conscious to enjoy. Grab a ribbon dancer and follow your Little Chef around the house to the beat of some great music. Experiment with lasso moves, waves, zigzags, and whatever Little Chef can invent.

1 to 2 ribbon dancing wands (also called ribbon streamers) per person
Music of choice

With the ribbon wand in hand, dance like nobody is watching! Talk about how much fun ribbons are and whether or not you could make a lasso or a wave out of a spinach ribbon!

✪ TODDLER SKILLS TIP: Always stay close to your little one when they are playing with ribbon wands. They are a wonderful, fun way to play, but could be dangerous without adult supervision.

Miso Ramen with Mixed Vegetables

SERVES 2 • **PREP TIME:** 15 MINUTES • **COOK TIME:** 4 MINUTES

Traditional ramen noodles have a history that predates the packaged stuff we ate in college. This fast and delicious recipe is great to make with your Little Chef, but also consider using it for meal prep for your own busy week. You can buy high-quality ramen noodle bricks, including many gluten-free options, online or at various cultural markets or health food stores. If you'd like a protein boost, add cubed firm tofu or cooked chicken or beef at step 4.

DAIRY-FREE, GLUTEN-FREE OPTIONAL, NUT-FREE, VEGAN, VEGETARIAN

¼ teaspoon diced garlic

2 teaspoons miso paste

1 tablespoon tahini

1 teaspoon soy sauce, tamari, or coconut amino acids

1 carrot

¼ cup spinach

¼ zucchini

¼ cup mushrooms

1 green onion

2 cups hot water

¼ brick dehydrated ramen noodles (or ½ cup noodles of your choice, cooked to al dente consistency)

½ cup mixed frozen veggies

1 teaspoon toasted sesame seeds (optional)

1. **SOUS CHEF:** Combine the garlic, miso, tahini, and soy sauce in a heat-safe, lidded container. Mix it into a paste. Set aside.

2. **EXECUTIVE CHEF:** Use a peeler to peel the carrot and then to cut it into ribbons. Set aside.

3. EXECUTIVE CHEF: Chop the spinach, zucchini, and mushrooms into small chunks and set aside.

4. EXECUTIVE CHEF: Chop the green onion and set aside.

5. ADULT STEP: Add the hot water to the paste and stir quickly until the paste is fully dissolved. Push the brick of dried noodles down into the water.

6. SOUS CHEF: Add the spinach, zucchini, mushrooms, and carrots to the top of the hot water.

7. ADULT STEP: Stir everything together. Cover and let sit for 4 minutes (or per noodle package instructions).

8. ADULT STEP: Add the frozen veggies to the hot water. They will warm up immediately as they cool down the soup for Little Chef!

9. LINE COOK: Sprinkle the green onion and sesame seeds (if using) on top and enjoy!

✪ **TODDLER SKILLS TIP:** Discuss the differences in veggies while cutting. How does a mushroom cut differently than spinach or carrots?

✪ **NUTRITION TIP:** Using frozen veggies to cool down soup is a favorite trick of mine. They cool without diluting the meal and boost both the flavor and the nutrition.

✪ **COOKING TIP:** Make this as a meal-prep option by using a heat-safe container: make your soup base paste at the bottom, stack your noodles on top, followed by the veggies. When it's lunchtime, just add water, let it sit for 4 minutes, and stir.

Chopstick Training

We can use food as a wonderful way to explore cultures not our own. It's fun to talk about how people eat in different areas of the world. In Northern Africa, it's common to use your fingers to eat. In many Asian countries, chopsticks are used. When first learning how to use chopsticks, it's best to use chopstick helpers. These can be fancy or very basic. When I was a kid, my father took the wrapper off the wooden chopsticks, rolled it into a ball, wedged it between the top of the two chopsticks, and bound it with a rubber band. It worked perfectly.

Mixed frozen veggies (either frozen or defrosted) or veggies from your soup recipe
Chopsticks
Chopstick helpers

1. Spread out the veggies on a plate or directly on the table.

2. Ask Little Chef if they can pick something up using only the chopsticks.

3. Have fun by creating challenges:

   ✿ How long can you hold the object in your chopsticks?

   ✿ Can you sort your veggies by color?

   ✿ Can you organize your veggies by size? By shape?

   ✿ Can we practice counting veggies as you lift and lower the pieces?

✪**MIX IT UP:** This will be easy for some and difficult for others. If you see that Little Chef is getting frustrated, take off the chopstick helpers. Use the chopsticks to create a frame, and then make a colorful picture inside the frame with the veggies.

Lunch Crunch Roll-Up

MAKES 1 ROLL-UP • **PREP TIME:** 10 MINUTES

This Lunch Crunch Roll-Up is creamy and crunchy and sweet and savory in every bite, providing a variety of taste experiences. Little Chef will love spreading the nut butter, sprinkling the Cheerios, and rolling the whole thing up.

....

DAIRY-FREE, GLUTEN-FREE OPTIONAL, MESSY HANDS, NUT-FREE OPTIONAL, VEGAN, VEGETARIAN

1 apple
1 lavash flatbread (or tortilla, naan, pita, or other flatbread)
¼ cup nut or seed butter
¼ cup chopped raisins or dried cranberries
¼ cup toasted sunflower seeds
¼ cup Cheerios
Pinch cinnamon

....

1. **ADULT STEP:** Cut the apple in half and core it.

2. **EXECUTIVE CHEF:** Cut the apple into matchsticks.

3. **SOUS CHEF:** Lay out the lavash and spread nut or seed butter over the whole surface.

4. **SOUS CHEF:** Lay apple match-sticks lengthwise down the center of the lavash.

5. **LINE COOK:** Sprinkle the raisins or cranberries, seeds, and cereal on top of the apples.

6. **SOUS CHEF:** Dust with a pinch of cinnamon.

7. **SOUS CHEF:** Roll up the lavash lengthwise.

8. **EXECUTIVE CHEF:** Cut the roll-up in half.

9. **ADULT STEP:** Serve immediately or wrap tightly and refrigerate.

✪ **TODDLER SKILLS TIP:** These matchsticks won't be lighting any fires—they are going to be all different shapes and sizes, and that's wonderful. Any amount of cutting will do the job.

✪ **SAFETY TIP:** Chop up raisins or dried cranberries because they are a choking hazard in their full form.

Practice Somersaults

Whether you call it a tumble, forward roll, or somersault, rolling is fun. Use the rolling action in the Lunch Crunch Roll-Up and teach your child how to tumble! You can teach them on a grassy hill, on a large foam wedge, or just on a soft, flat surface.

....

1. Start with your feet solid on the ground. Spread your legs to make a triangle.

2. Place your hands on the ground right in between your feet.

3. Tuck your head to look through your legs at the wall behind. You can place a target on the wall for your child to use for focus.

4. Tuck and roll!

✪**TODDLER SKILLS TIP:** Many gyms start teaching children forward rolls as early as 7 months of age. According to My Gym Maitland, forward rolls teach a child body awareness and control, eye tracking (an important pre-reading skill), bilateral coordination, development of core strength, confidence, and fun.

✪**SAFETY TIP:** The top of the head should not touch the ground because it can put stress on the child's neck. The back of the head or the top of the neck should be the point connecting with the ground for maximum safety.

Lettuce Wraps with Marinated Tofu

MAKES 8 LETTUCE WRAPS • **PREP TIME:** 30 MINUTES • **COOK TIME:** 30 MINUTES

Lettuce wraps are refreshing and delicious, and finding another fun use for a colorful vegetable is a great side benefit. You can incorporate lettuce wraps into many different types of dishes, boosting the fun factor at any meal. Look for lettuce or cabbage that has some substance to it. A flimsy lettuce leaf won't hold your meal quite as well and may be frustrating for little hands.

....

DAIRY-FREE, GLUTEN-FREE OPTIONAL, MESSY HANDS, NUT FREE, VEGAN OPTIONAL, VEGETARIAN

1 block firm tofu

3 tablespoons honey (or maple syrup)

1 tablespoon sesame oil

2 tablespoons soy sauce (or tamari)

2 garlic cloves, diced

¼ teaspoon ground ginger (or ½ teaspoon fresh, grated)

Olive oil (optional), for coating the baking sheet

1 large carrot

¼ head red cabbage

1 mango

2 green onions

1 head romaine, Boston bibb, or iceberg lettuce or white cabbage

1 cup mung bean sprouts

....

1. **ADULT STEP:** Drain and press the tofu.

2. **EXECUTIVE CHEF:** Measure out the sauce ingredients: honey, sesame oil, soy sauce, garlic, and ginger.

3. **SOUS CHEF:** Combine the sauce ingredients in a small bowl and stir.

CONTINUED →

Lettuce Wraps with Marinated Tofu CONTINUED

4. **EXECUTIVE CHEF:** Cube the tofu into blocks roughly the size of the tip of your pinkie finger.

5. **SOUS CHEF:** Marinate the tofu in half of the sauce and reserve the rest for dipping.

6. **EXECUTIVE CHEF:** Prepare a baking sheet by lining it with a sheet of parchment paper or lightly coating with olive oil.

7. **ADULT STEP:** Preheat the oven to 425°F. Lay out the tofu on the prepared baking sheet and bake for 10 minutes on each side. Let it cool.

8. **EXECUTIVE CHEF:** Peel the carrot into ribbons or shred in the food processor.

9. **EXECUTIVE CHEF:** Chiffonade the cabbage by cutting into shred-like strips.

10. **EXECUTIVE CHEF:** Cut the mango into strips.

11. **EXECUTIVE CHEF:** Chop the green onions.

12. **EXECUTIVE CHEF:** Open the lettuce and lay out 8 to 10 whole leaves on your workspace.

13. **LINE COOK:** Add the mung bean sprouts, carrot, cabbage, mango, green onions, and cooled tofu to the lettuce cups.

14. **SOUS CHEF:** Use the remaining sauce as a dip or add it directly to the lettuce wraps.

✪ **TODDLER SKILLS TIP:** This is a messy dish to eat, even for adults. Discuss the mess factor with Little Chef before creating the dish, before serving the dish, and when you sit down to eat. If Little Chef seems bothered by a lettuce wrap that isn't quite holding together, consider making a mess of your own and enjoying the delicious mess together.

✪ **MIX IT UP:** Try making lettuce wraps out of a different dinner—it's great for using up leftovers. Consider chicken and veggies, leftover meatloaf, or even Thanksgiving turkey!

Be a Bunny with Lettuce Ears

Getting goofy is a valuable skill for kids and adults of all ages. When we develop the skill to turn the mundane into the silly, we develop an important stress-management coping mechanism. When we can join our kids in this silly time, we create a space of comfort and safety, increasing the chances that they will feel comfortable coming to us with the less-silly questions or obstacles in life.

Lettuce or cabbage leaves (at least 2 per person)

....

1. Lay out the lettuce leaves.

2. As your Little Chef fun questions:

✿ Practice your bunny nose. Can you scrunch your nose like a bunny?

✿ Put up your ears! Can you make bunny ears out of lettuce? Are your ears up or down? Do they move from side to side? Do they help you hear better?

✪ **MIX IT UP:** Bunnies love carrots. Can you hide some real or fake carrots around the house for you and your Little Chef Bunny to find?

Baked Chickpea, Sweet Potato, and Spinach Empanadas

MAKES 8 EMPANADAS • **PREP TIME:** 25 MINUTES • **COOK TIME:** 20 MINUTES

Empanadas are pastry turnovers common in Southern European, Latin American, Indonesian, and Filipino cultures. The concept of handheld pies filled with sweet or savory filling has made an appearance in many places across the globe due to their ease, versatility, and convenience. Enjoy this recipe as it's written, or use the dough to deliciously pack up leftovers from a previous meal. You can even add garlic or cinnamon to the dough to match your chosen filling. My favorite fillings are meatloaf and mashed potatoes, slow cooker salsa chicken, or sautéed spinach and feta cheese.

···

DAIRY-FREE OPTIONAL, GLUTEN-FREE OPTIONAL, MESSY HANDS, NUT-FREE, VEGAN OPTIONAL, VEGETARIAN

Nonstick cooking spray

1⅓ cup whole-wheat flour or gluten-free flour

1 teaspoon baking powder

1 teaspoon salt, divided

½ cup aquafaba (the liquid from a can of garbanzo beans), milk, or milk substitute

¼ cup olive oil, divided

1 cup cooked and peeled sweet potato

1 cup cooked garbanzo beans, rinsed and drained

½ teaspoon garlic powder

2 teaspoons cumin

⅓ cup green onion

1 cup fresh spinach or kale

Soy milk, for glazing

···

1. **ADULT STEP:** Preheat the oven to 400°F.

2. **EXECUTIVE CHEF:** Coat a baking sheet with cooking spray.

3. **LINE COOK:** Combine the flour, baking powder, and ½ teaspoon of salt in a large bowl.

4. **SOUS CHEF:** Slowly add the aquafaba and 2 teaspoons of olive oil, mixing until just combined.

5. **EXECUTIVE CHEF:** Form the dough into a ball, cover, and let rest for about 10 minutes. The dough should be elastic but not sticky.

6. **LINE COOK:** In a medium bowl, mash the sweet potato, beans, garlic, cumin, and remaining 2 tablespoons of olive oil.

7. **EXECUTIVE CHEF:** Dice the green onion and chop the spinach.

8. **LINE COOK:** Add the green onion and spinach to the sweet potato mixture.

9. **EXECUTIVE CHEF** (with some assistance): Separate the dough into 8 balls and roll with a rolling pin into thin circles, about 6 inches in diameter.

10. **SOUS CHEF:** Fill half of each circle and fold dough over, creating a half-moon shape.

11. **EXECUTIVE CHEF:** Pinch the dough shut with a fork and place on the prepared baking sheet.

12. **LINE COOK:** Glaze each empanada with soy milk.

13. **ADULT STEP:** Cut three small diagonal slits on the top of each empanada to let steam escape.

14. **ADULT STEP:** Bake 18 to 20 minutes, or until browned. Let cool for about 10 minutes.

✪ **TODDLER SKILLS TIP:** Some actions require team effort. For example, when dicing the green onions, Little Chef can begin, then the parent can dice and pass the green onions back to Little Chef for a final pass. Allowing your little one to have the final say will result in adequately diced green onions with a side of boosted confidence.

Start an Eggshell Garden

Starting a garden is a sure-fire way to get kids involved in their food. Gardening includes all the activities that come naturally to children: getting messy, spraying water, and patience. You got me—I added that last one. But truthfully, gardening can help a child develop patience as they see something miraculous happening each morning. I'll never forget the time a client told me about a recipe that required green onions. She didn't have green onions in her garden, so she bought a bunch and threw them under a bush. The kids went hunting, and what do you know? They found green onions for her recipe.

Eggs

Shoebox (or similar)

Sharp pin or tack

Soil (potting soil or dirt from your yard)

Seeds (tomato, lettuce, cucumber, carrot, herbs, or something else that grows well in your location and climate)

Spray bottle

Magnifying glass (optional but fun)

1. Remove the eggs from the shells (and make some breakfast!), wash the shells, and then boil them in a pot for three minutes. Lay out to dry.

2. Use a pin or thumbtack to carefully create a drainage hole in the bottom of the shell.

3. Fill the base of a shoebox with soil and place your eggshell there, making sure it is stable.

4. Have Little Chef fill the eggshell about three-quarters full with soil and sprinkle seeds on top.

5. Dampen the seeds and place your eggshell pot in a sunny place. To avoid overwatering, give Little Chef a spray bottle to spray water onto the shells.

6. Continue to keep the soil moist with regular spraying. Wait for the seeds to sprout. This should happen within a week or so. Use a magnifying glass to monitor (and enjoy) growth.

7. When you're ready to transfer your eggshell garden into the ground, dig an eggshell-sized hole in the ground, crack the bottom on the eggshell, and place it in the ground. The shell itself will act as a fertilizer as the egg decomposes and the roots push into the ground.

✪ **MIX IT UP:** For added fun, use a soil-safe marker to draw faces on your eggshells or to label what you've planted. Have Little Chef draw pictures of the seedlings as they sprout and grow. Talk about what you're growing and how you might like to eat it when it's ready.

Fun with Lunch and Dinner   **73**

Baked Veggie Egg Rolls

MAKES 8 EGG ROLLS • **PREP TIME:** 15 MINUTES • **COOK TIME:** 15 MINUTES

According to *Chop Suey: A Cultural History of Chinese Food in the United States*, the first egg rolls found in the United States are thought to have come from one of two Chinese restaurants in New York. The egg roll that is familiar to us was inspired by a traditional Chinese spring roll but was altered to appeal to American tastes and available ingredients. The first official mention of the egg roll was in Henry Low's 1938 book *Cook at Home in Chinese*. It's fascinating to see how recipes change with migration of people, spices, and plants. Fried food has amazing flavor and texture, but it can be very difficult to involve Little Chef in the act of frying. These baked egg rolls combine the delicious, familiar flavor with a method of cooking that's friendlier to little hands.

....

DAIRY-FREE, GLUTEN-FREE OPTIONAL, MESSY HANDS, NUT-FREE, VEGAN, VEGETARIAN

1 package egg roll skins

Nonstick cooking spray

2 teaspoons diced garlic

½ teaspoon ground ginger (or 1½ teaspoons fresh, grated)

1 teaspoon maple syrup or honey

2 teaspoons soy sauce

2 teaspoons sesame oil

⅛ teaspoon freshly ground black pepper

¾ teaspoon kosher salt

1 teaspoon rice wine vinegar

1 large carrot

⅓ bell pepper

3 green onions

2 cups shredded cabbage or coleslaw mix

½ cup small pineapple chunks (plus extra for "tasting")

....

1. **ADULT STEP:** If necessary, defrost the egg roll skins, following the package directions.

2. **ADULT STEP:** Preheat the oven to 400°F.

3. **EXECUTIVE CHEF:** Liberally coat a baking sheet with cooking spray. Set aside.

4. **LINE COOK:** Mix the garlic, ginger, maple syrup, soy sauce, sesame oil, black pepper, salt, and vinegar in a small bowl.

5. **EXECUTIVE CHEF:** Shred the carrot either by peeling into strips with a peeler or by using the shredding attachment on a food processor. Thinly slice the bell pepper. Chop the green onions.

6. **LINE COOK:** Place the cabbage to a large bowl, pour the sauce mixture over it, and mix.

7. **LINE COOK:** Add the carrot, bell pepper, green onions, and pineapple to the bowl and mix well.

8. **EXECUTIVE CHEF** (with some adult modeling or assistance): Lay one egg roll skin on a flat, dry surface. Add about 2 tablespoons of the veggie mix to the center of the egg roll skin in a straight line. Fold the egg roll skin from the bottom, making a tight tube of the mixture. Fold the sides in and continue to roll upward. Dip your finger in water and lightly wet the top corner of the sheet. Finish rolling upward and place it seam-side down on the prepared baking sheet.

Spray liberally with nonstick cooking spray. Continue until all the mixture is used.

9. **ADULT STEP:** Bake for 7 minutes, flip, and cook for another 7 minutes, or until golden.

✪ **TODDLER SKILLS TIP:** Mixing is a great introduction to cooking. It seems simple and straightforward, but as the ingredients and the flavors combine, something new is created. This skill is appropriate even for the littlest chef. Be sure to watch their face as the colors and textures combine to form something new.

✪ **NUTRITION TIP:** Allow Little Chef to taste as you go. When we made these at Toddler Test Kitchen™, the kids were even sampling the raw egg roll skins! The freedom to taste as you go will help them gain familiarity with each individual ingredient. If you end up running low on a specific ingredient, the recipe will still work out just fine.

Create a Toddler Obstacle Course

Create a mini American Gladiator course for Little Chef. Use the "roll" part of the egg roll for inspiration, including forward rolls (page 66), toddler tunnels, or both! Little Chef will use their body in different ways, improving their hand-eye coordination and more. According to an article published by Michigan State University, movement can help "increase memory, perception, language, attention, emotion and even decision making. When language is combined with movement, learning increases 90 percent."

Toddler tunnel tent, store-bought or homemade

Trampoline

Baby pool

Balance beam (or line of duct tape to represent balance beam)

Sprinkler

Slide

Bubbles

Plastic rings

Balls

Laundry basket

Painter's tape

Couch cushions

OBSTACLE COURSE OPTIONS:

TODDLER TUNNEL: Encourage your toddler to crawl through or slide over your tunnel.

TRAMPOLINE: Complete as many jumps as you feel your child is capable of.

BABY POOL: Fill with water or plastic balls.

BALANCE BEAM (OR LINE OF DUCT TAPE): Walk or crawl on the beam or line.

SPRINKLER: Run through, jump through, or forward roll through the sprinkler.

SLIDE: Slide down, run up, or crawl under the slide.

BUBBLES: Create a bubble blowing station or use it to celebrate the end of the course.

PLASTIC RINGS: Toss the rings, place them on the floor, and have your child step in each one toward the next station.

LAUNDRY BASKET: Create a ball toss with the laundry basket as the goal.

PAINTER'S TAPE: Tape back and forth across a hallway like a spider's web, and have your Little Chef crawl underneath or walk over the lines.

COUCH CUSHIONS: Create a mountain for climbing or a space for landing jumps.

⊛ **TODDLER SKILLS TIP:** Stick with obstacles that will challenge your child but not frustrate them so much that it isn't fun. It should be difficult, but not too far above their ability.

Cheese and Vegetable Quesadilla

MAKES 2 QUESADILLAS · **PREP TIME:** 10 MINUTES · **COOK TIME:** 10 MINUTES

What is more classic and comforting than the combination of cheese and bread? This simple quesadilla is a wonderful base for color, crunch, and satisfaction. Start out with the basic cheese and tortilla, and from there you can build a delicious rainbow. Tortillas come in a range of sizes, so you may need more or less cheese depending on your tortilla size. Use an electric griddle for this recipe if you have it, and see the Toddler Skills Tip for instructions. An electric griddle allows adults to change a diaper or clean up a mess and feel confident that food won't burn, it provides an even cooking environment, and it's more stable than a pan, which makes it safer for Little Chef.

DAIRY-FREE OPTIONAL, GLUTEN-FREE OPTIONAL, NUT-FREE, VEGAN OPTIONAL, VEGETARIAN

1 **green onion** (optional)
½ **bell pepper** (optional)
½ **cup spinach** (optional)
4 **(10-inch) corn, flour, or combination tortillas**
1 **cup grated cheddar cheese**
¼ **cup corn niblets** (optional)
4 **tablespoons butter, olive oil, or avocado oil, divided**
2 **tablespoons sour cream, for garnish**
2 **tablespoons salsa, for garnish**
2 **tablespoons guacamole, for garnish**

1. **EXECUTIVE CHEF:** If using, chop the green onion, bell pepper, and spinach, creating a small pile of each vegetable.

2. **SOUS CHEF:** Lay out two tortillas on a clean, flat surface.

3. **LINE COOK:** Sprinkle the cheese on one of the tortillas, making sure to cover most of the tortilla.

4. **LINE COOK:** If using, sprinkle the green onion, bell pepper, spinach, and corn on top of the cheese.

5. **LINE COOK:** Place the second tortilla on top of the first.

6. **ADULT STEP:** Heat a pan over low heat and add 1 tablespoon of butter. Cook the set of tortillas for about 2 minutes, or until the bottom tortilla begins to brown. Use a spatula to lift the edge and check. Flip the tortilla and cook the other side the same way, adding 1 more tablespoon of butter to cook that side.

7. **ADULT STEP:** Repeat with the second set of tortillas.

8. **ADULT STEP:** Allow the quesadillas to cool; then use a pizza slicer to cut them into quarters, sixths, or eighths.

9. **LINE COOK:** Top each slice with more veggies, sour cream, salsa, or guacamole, and enjoy!

✪**TODDLER SKILLS TIP:** The electric griddle is a safer option if you're up for the challenge of including Little Chef in flipping the quesadilla. Heat the griddle to 300°F at step 6. You may use butter or oil or cook directly on the cooktop.

✪**PLAYTIME!** Can you make binoculars out of tortillas and play "I Spy"?

Stretch Like Cheese Yoga Poses

According to a blog from Harvard Medical School, yoga and other mindful activities offer psychological benefits including improved focus, memory, self-esteem, behavior, and academic performance; they can even reduce anxiety and stress. Get down on the floor and giggle with your child as you stretch like the cheese in your quesadilla!

Calming music
Mat, rug, or carpeted floor

ACTIVITY OPTIONS:

UPSIDE-DOWN TRIANGLE

1. Stand with feet apart and take a deep breath.

2. Blow your breath out slowly as you place your hands on the floor between your feet.

3. Let your head hang down and breathe.

STRETCH

4. Sit on your bottom with legs extended into a large V.

5. Lean over to the right and try to touch your shin or your foot or even grab your toes.

6. Repeat on the left.

BUTTERFLY

7. From the previous pose, bring your feet together so the soles of your feet are touching.

8. Flap your knees up and down like a butterfly.

TREE POSE

9. Stand on one leg, bringing the opposite foot to your shin.

10. Raise your hands up into the air.

11. Try to look up at the ceiling.

12. Now try with the other leg.

✪ **MIX IT UP:** Ask your child to play yoga teacher, instructing you in new poses of their own creation!

One-Pan Chicken, Potatoes, and Broccoli

SERVES 6 · **PREP TIME:** 15 MINUTES · **COOK TIME:** 35 MINUTES

One-pan recipes are essential for busy evenings. They are also a great starting point for including Little Chef in the creation of a dinner that the whole family can enjoy together. The confidence boost Little Chef will have when seeing parents, siblings, and other loved ones eat the delicious dinner they made will be evident on Little Chef's face.

....

DAIRY-FREE, GLUTEN-FREE, MESSY HANDS, NUT-FREE

Nonstick cooking spray

2 pounds red potatoes (about 6 medium)

1 large onion

1¼ teaspoons salt, divided

1 teaspoon dried rosemary, crushed, divided (or 3 teaspoons fresh rosemary)

1 teaspoon freshly ground black pepper, divided

1 head broccoli or bag of florets

3 tablespoons olive oil

4 garlic cloves, minced (or 1 tablespoon diced garlic from a jar)

½ teaspoon sweet paprika

6 bone-in chicken thighs (about 2¼ pounds), or alternately the same amount of salmon

....

1. **ADULT STEP:** Preheat the oven to 425°F.

2. **EXECUTIVE CHEF:** Coat a baking sheet with cooking spray. Set aside.

3. **ADULT STEP:** Halve the potatoes and the onion to create a flat surface for Little Chef to continue cutting.

4. **EXECUTIVE CHEF:** Quarter the potatoes. Quarter each half of the onion and separate the pieces.

5. **EXECUTIVE CHEF:** Measure out ¾ teaspoon of salt, ½ teaspoon of rosemary, and ½ teaspoon of pepper. Take a moment to smoosh some rosemary between your fingers and smell it.

6. **LINE COOK:** In a large bowl, combine the potatoes, onion, broccoli, oil, garlic, and spice mixture. Mix well.

7. **EXECUTIVE CHEF** (with adult assistance): Transfer the vegetable mixture to the baking sheet.

8. **LINE COOK:** In a small bowl, mix the paprika and the remaining salt, rosemary, and pepper. Sprinkle the chicken with the paprika mixture and arrange over the vegetables.

9. **ADULT STEP:** Roast until a meat thermometer inserted into the chicken reads an internal temperature of 165°F and the vegetables are tender, 30 to 35 minutes. Remove the pan from the oven and let cool.

✪ **TODDLER SKILLS TIP:** It's very difficult to prepare raw meat with children. It's critical to speak to Little Chef ahead of time, explaining how important it is to wash hands carefully and to keep their hands away from their mouth while cooking. If your child hasn't yet developed that level of focus, you can either choose to focus on the non-meat steps or select a different recipe for the time being.

✪ **MIX IT UP:** Make this recipe with salmon instead of chicken. Cook the vegetables for 15 minutes; then add salmon to the pan and cook for 20 to 25 minutes, or until it reaches an internal temperature of 145°F.

Spiced Play Dough

This is a fun and creative way to introduce kids to the scents and colors of new seasonings. Each batch is intended to feature a single seasoning. See the tip at the end for more spice suggestions. If you can't find ground rosemary, grind dried rosemary with a mortar and pestle or in a coffee grinder.

⚙ MIX IT UP: For the most fun, make multiple batches and compare the color, smell, and texture of the different dough balls. Consider 1 to 2 tablespoons mild mustard powder, 1 tablespoon ground cinnamon, 2 to 3 tablespoons ground cumin, 1½ tablespoons ground turmeric, 1 to 2 tablespoons cocoa powder, or 1 teaspoon paprika.

½ cup all-purpose flour
½ cup water
1 tablespoon salt
1 teaspoon cream of tartar
2 tablespoons ground rosemary

1. Have Little Chef add the flour, water, salt, and cream of tartar to a saucepan and mix well until smooth.

2. Add the ground rosemary and mix well.

3. Heat over low-medium, stirring constantly, until the mixture forms into a ball.

4. Place the dough on wax paper and let cool for 20 to 30 minutes; then knead until smooth.

Super Beet Cookies
PAGE 88

CHAPTER FIVE

Exploring with Sides and Snacks

Make Your Own Beet Stamp
PAGE 90
▼

Super Beet Cookies

MAKES 8 COOKIES • **PREP TIME:** 20 MINUTES • **COOK TIME:** 20 MINUTES

These vibrant cookies are great for Valentine's Day, holidays, and all the days in between. Beets provide a vibrant color to match their amazing nutrition. This dough is thick and requires a lot of kneading, but it also feels like play dough, so have fun with it. See if you can make cookies shaped like hearts, ruby red slippers, or even beets!

....

DAIRY-FREE, GLUTEN-FREE OPTIONAL, MESSY HANDS, NUT-FREE, VEGAN OPTIONAL, VEGETARIAN

Nonstick cooking spray (optional)

¾ cup shredded fresh beets (about 1 small fresh beet)

1 cup whole-wheat pastry flour (or all-purpose white flour)

½ teaspoon baking powder

¼ teaspoon cinnamon

¼ teaspoon salt

¼ cup melted unsalted butter or light oil, such as olive oil, avocado oil, or coconut oil

3 Medjool dates, smooshed with a fork

¼ teaspoon vanilla

....

1. **ADULT STEP:** Preheat the oven to 400°F.

2. **EXECUTIVE CHEF:** Line a baking sheet with parchment paper or coat with cooking spray. Set aside.

3. **LINE COOK:** Add the beets to the food processor for shredding (or **ADULT STEP:** Shred beets with a handheld shredder).

4. **LINE COOK:** In a large bowl, combine the flour, baking powder, cinnamon, and salt. Add the shredded beets and stir.

5. **LINE COOK:** Add the butter, smooshed dates, and vanilla.

6. **LINE COOK:** Knead until the dough is smooth and the consistency of play dough.

7. **SOUS CHEF:** Place the ball of dough on a sheet of parchment paper. Cover with a second sheet of parchment and roll out to about ½ inch thick.

8. **SOUS CHEF:** Cut out fun shapes with a cookie cutter or the rim of a glass.

9. **SOUS CHEF:** Place the cookies on the prepared baking sheet about 2 inches apart.

10. **ADULT STEP:** Place in the oven and bake for 15 to 17 minutes.

11. **ADULT STEP:** Let cool for about 10 minutes and enjoy!

✪ **TODDLER SKILLS TIP:** If Little Chef is getting tired of kneading, play a game where you knead and pass. Create a ball and roll it to Little Chef, and then have Little Chef create a fun shape and roll (or clunk) it back to you.

✪ **NUTRITION TIP:** If Little Chef really likes these cookies, you'll see evidence in the diaper or toilet the next day! If you see red, keep in mind what Little Chef ate.

Make Your Own Beet Stamp

Create beet-utiful art with your beet! Can you make a dinosaur? An initial? A family crest? Have fun with your very own custom stamp!

Raw beet
Cookie cutter
Paring knife
Paper

⭐ **MIX IT UP:** You can also do this with a bunch of celery, bound together. You'll need to add some paint or ink to the list of supplies for this.

1. Take a raw beet, cut off the greens, and cut it in half widthwise. Save the greens for juicing, sautéing, or to add to soup.

2. Use a cookie cutter to cut a shape outline into the beet; then use a paring knife to carefully cut around your design.

3. Have Little Chef take their new beet stamp and use it to make beautiful art on a blank sheet of paper!

Hulk Muffins

MAKES 12 LARGE MUFFINS · **PREP TIME:** 15 MINUTES, PLUS 30 MINUTES TO COOL
COOK TIME: 20 MINUTES

Kids are attracted to bright colors, and these muffins won't disappoint. They are easy to make and nutritious, and they freeze and travel well. If you're using a non-dairy alternative, be sure to use soy milk or another thin option. Canned coconut milk will not work in this recipe.

•••••••••••••••••••••••••••••••••

DAIRY-FREE OPTIONAL, GLUTEN-FREE OPTIONAL, NUT-FREE, VEGAN OPTIONAL, VEGETARIAN

2 cups whole-wheat flour
(or 1 cup oat flour and
1 cup gluten-free flour)

2 teaspoons baking powder

½ teaspoon baking soda

1½ teaspoons ground cinnamon

½ teaspoon salt

¼ cup olive oil or avocado oil

¾ cup milk or milk alternative

10 Medjool dates,
pitted and soaked

6 ounces fresh spinach

1 to 2 mashed bananas

2 teaspoons vanilla extract

•••••••••••••••••••••••••••••••••

1. **ADULT STEP:** Preheat the oven to 350°F.

2. **EXECUTIVE CHEF:** Line a 12-cup muffin tin with liners or spray with cooking spray.

3. **LINE COOK:** Whisk together the flour, baking powder, baking soda, cinnamon, and salt in a large bowl, and set aside.

4. **SOUS CHEF:** Add the olive oil, milk, dates, spinach, bananas, and vanilla extract to a blender and blend until smooth.

CONTINUED →

Hulk Muffins CONTINUED

5. **LINE COOK:** Pour the pureed mixture into the dry mixture and fold together until just incorporated.

6. **EXECUTIVE CHEF:** Fill the muffin cups until about two-thirds full.

7. **ADULT STEP:** Bake for 18 to 20 minutes until a toothpick comes out clean. Remove and let cool for about 30 minutes.

✪ TODDLER SKILLS TIP: If you are including Little Chef in step 4, be sure to position the blender at a height that works for both of you. Little Chef should be able to drop ingredients into the blender without access to the blades but also without having to stand on their tippy toes.

✪ PLAYTIME! Play up the Hulk angle by flexing your biceps for each other! Be sure to be extra goofy. Or, while the muffins are in the oven or cooling, lay out a few spinach leaves, banana slices, and dates. Use the ingredients to make silly faces! Can you show me happy? Sad? Excited?

Spinach Construction Site

For many kids, trucks and loud noises make everything more fun! Including favorite toys when trying something new can make the experience a bit more familiar. Inspired by Anna Thompson, a children's occupational therapist, this activity invites Little Chef's fleet of construction trucks to join in the fun. If construction trucks are not your child's interest, change up the activity to include Little Chef's favorite toy. For a doll and tea set, float some chopped spinach in water and have a tea party with cucumber sandwiches. Use race cars to create a track with spinach obstacles. Or build a castle with some LEGOs and see how much spinach you can float inside. Ask Little Chef: Can you fit one cup? Two cups?

Spinach
Construction trucks

....

1. Gather any construction trucks your child may have and create a construction site with spinach leaves.

2. Ask your child some questions:

   ❀ Can the truck pick up spinach and deliver it from one side of the counter to the other?

   ❀ Can the truck roll over a big heap of spinach leaves?

   ❀ What sound might the truck make as it crunches on spinach?

✪ MIX IT UP: Let Little Chef lead the way! Put out a pile of spinach and ask, "How can we have fun with this today?"

Easy Blender Dips

Kids tend to love dips for a few reasons: They love being in charge, dips are often colorful, and dips lend themselves well to experimentation. There is no commitment with a dip—you dip once, and if you don't like it, you don't have to experience that sensation again. Dips also keep well and are versatile, so if Little Chef isn't thrilled by the dip of the day, you can easily pack it up and repurpose it as a salad dressing, sandwich spread, or condiment. They are also nutritious! For example, two tablespoons of sparlick provide 12 percent of an adult's daily requirement for vitamin A, 16 percent vitamin C, and 154 percent vitamin K, all based on the RDI. Consider making all three dips for Little Chef to try. Do they taste better on a cracker, a slice of tomato, or on a finger?

....

DAIRY-FREE, GLUTEN-FREE, NUT-FREE, VEGAN, VEGETARIAN

✪ **TO MAKE ALL DIP VARIATIONS:** LINE COOK: In a blender or food processor, combine all ingredients and blend until the desired texture is reached.

Hummus

MAKES 2 CUPS • **PREP TIME:** 10 MINUTES

Hummus has been a staple dish in the Middle East for centuries. It can be found at breakfast, lunch, dinner, and snacks. It is considered the ultimate condiment, providing delicious flavor, creamy texture, and a good dose of fiber, protein, anti-inflammatory fat, naturally occurring folate, and more.

....

15 ounces canned garbanzo beans, drained and rinsed

⅓ cup tahini

2½ tablespoons lemon juice (or to taste)

2 garlic cloves (or 3 if you're feeling adventurous)

2 tablespoons olive oil

⅛ teaspoon cumin

Pinch kosher salt

¼ cup seltzer (or to desired texture)

Vegan Ricotta

MAKES 2 CUPS • **PREP TIME:** 10 MINUTES

This creamy and delicious vegan ricotta uses tofu as a base. Tofu is inexpensive and widely available. It's a wonderful source of protein and calcium, essential for growing muscles and bones. Use this as a dip or in your favorite pasta dish!

1 block firm tofu, drained and pressed

1 tablespoon olive oil

1 tablespoon lemon juice

¾ teaspoon kosher salt

2 garlic cloves, diced

1 teaspoon dried rosemary

1 teaspoon dried oregano

1 teaspoon dried basil

2 cups raw spinach

Sparlick

MAKES 1 CUP • **PREP TIME:** 10 MINUTES

Sparlick, also called sparslic, or simply parsley garlic dip, is similar to many recipes found in and around Italy and Greece. In this form, it appears connected to the Chabad Hasidic community, but it isn't associated with any specific holiday.

1 bunch fresh parsley (2 ounces)

2 garlic cloves raw, chopped

⅓ cup olive oil

½ teaspoon kosher salt

Squeeze of lemon, plus more to taste (optional)

✪ **TODDLER SKILLS TIP:**
Although the **EXECUTIVE CHEF** will do a great job pouring liquids into the blender, the **LINE COOK** might appreciate the opportunity to put the lid on the blender and be in charge of the buttons.

Do the Dip Finger Painting

Getting messy is such an important part of childhood. Dips provide a wonderful opportunity for interacting with different textures. Positive interaction with food doesn't have to include a bite, and often it doesn't. It's all about the smile.

2 to 3 dips of different colors
White paper plate or
piece of paper

1. Give Little Chef a white paper plate or blank piece of paper and dips.

2. Ask Little Chef to draw a face, a heart, a rainbow, or maybe a race car!

⭐ **TODDLER SKILLS TIP:**
According to Dr. Rebecca Chicot, child development expert, toddlers often mimic what they see their parents doing. If the child sees the parent tidying up constantly and making sad faces when the child creates a mess, the child may become averse to mess. You can help Little Chef find a happy medium by getting into some messy play yourself. Join your little one in creating something fun and messy. You might start this activity with a sponge rather than fingers, and slowly progress to the full finger-painting activity.

Homemade Berry Soda

MAKES 2 (8-OUNCE) SERVINGS • **PREP TIME:** 2 MINUTES

Who doesn't love a refreshing, colorful beverage? This homemade soda can be thrown together and served with lunch, or it can be dressed up for a tea party. Berries provide color and flavor and an amazing amount of antioxidants and fiber—supporting both the immune system and overall health.

DAIRY-FREE, GLUTEN-FREE, NUT-FREE, VEGAN, VEGETARIAN

2 cups club soda or seltzer
¼ cup frozen berry mix
2 clear cups
2 fancy straws

1. **LINE COOK:** Place 2 tablespoons of frozen berry mix at the bottom of each clear cup.

2. **SOUS CHEF:** Pour 1 cup of club soda over the top of the berries.

3. Add a fancy straw to each cup and enjoy!

✪ **TODDLER SKILLS TIP:** Sometimes bags of frozen produce freeze into a block. Be sure to break up the frozen berries before asking Little Chef to scoop them.

✪ **NUTRITION TIP:** Both fiber and hydration can help with constipation concerns. If that is a current obstacle for your child, this recipe is a wonderful addition to any meal or snack!

Colorful Bubbles

Inspired by MamaPlusOne.com, this activity takes backyard bubbles to the next level by adding in some color! Match the colors of your bubbles to the colors in your Homemade Berry Soda for added fun. Be sure Little Chef is wearing old clothes or a swimsuit because food coloring can stain.

4 bubble jars or tall, cylindrical containers
1¼ cup room-temperature water
2 tablespoons sugar
⅓ cup dishwashing soap
Food coloring
Bubble wands

1. In an old bubble jar or other tall, thin container, mix the water and sugar until the sugar is fully dissolved.

2. Slowly add dishwashing soap, stirring slowly until incorporated. Avoid creating suds.

3. Pour ⅓ cup of the mixture into each of remaining containers and add food coloring as desired, about 8 drops per container.

4. Use bubble wands to create beautiful colorful bubbles!

⭐ **MIX IT UP:** Ask Little Chef if they can blow an apple bubble, a blueberry bubble, or an orange bubble. Ask them what their favorite color is and to name the kinds of food that are also that color.

Cinnamon Sweet Potato Fries

SERVES 8 · **PREP TIME:** 15 MINUTES · **COOK TIME:** 35 MINUTES

Sweet potatoes are versatile and delicious. They provide important fiber (particularly if the skin is left on), vitamin A, and vitamin C as well as a high antioxidant level that helps promote health and well-being. For younger babies, avoid a crunchy fry, so it is easy to chew, by thickly cutting the sweet potatoes or cooking them until just soft.

DAIRY-FREE, GLUTEN-FREE, NUT-FREE, VEGAN OPTIONAL, VEGETARIAN

2 tablespoons olive oil or melted butter, plus more to coat the baking sheet

2 pounds sweet potatoes

1 tablespoon cornstarch (optional)

½ teaspoon kosher salt

Pinch cinnamon

1. **ADULT STEP:** Preheat the oven to 425°F.

2. **EXECUTIVE CHEF:** Prepare the baking sheet by lightly coating it with olive oil.

3. **LINE COOK:** Wash and scrub the sweet potatoes until the skin is clean.

4. **EXECUTIVE CHEF** (with assistance): Cut the potatoes into a fry shape, around ¼ inch wide and ¼ inch thick.

5. **LINE COOK:** Place the fries into a large bowl or plastic bag.

CONTINUED →

Cinnamon Sweet Potato Fries CONTINUED

6. **LINE COOK:** Toss the fries in cornstarch (if using) and salt; then lay flat on the prepared baking sheet in a single layer.

7. **SOUS CHEF:** Drizzle with the olive oil or butter; then sprinkle with the cinnamon and toss to coat.

8. **ADULT STEP:** Bake fries for 20 minutes; then flip and bake for another 15 minutes.

✪ **MIX IT UP:** You can substitute carrots for the sweet potato. Follow the same instructions, but at step 8, bake the carrots at 350°F for 12 minutes. Consider replacing cinnamon with Parmesan cheese or garlic for a different flavor experience.

Fun with Mr. Potato Head

Some of the most classic toys are still the best. Mr. Potato Head allows for fun with a vegetable! Having fun with food is key to creating a familiar and friendly table environment. When we introduce a fun activity that replicates a food item without asking the child to taste it, we allow the child to fully experience the fun aspect without the worry. If you don't have the classic version, you can recreate the best parts, either with a potato drawing or by using a raw potato with stick-on eyes and other accessories.

Mr. Potato Head or 1 white or sweet potato
Paper
Scissors
Crayons
Tape or glue (optional)

1. On the paper, draw the outline of a potato.

2. Ask Little Chef to arrange cutouts of eyes, ears, glasses, legs, lips, and even accessories, arranging them on the sweet potato or drawing.

⭐ **MIX IT UP:** Go rogue by introducing other vegetables for even more fun! Consider Ms. Beet or Kid Kudzu!

Spiral Squash

SERVES 2 • **PREP TIME:** 15 MINUTES

Noodles lend themselves to fun with their squiggly and long shape. These veggie noodles bump up that fun with vibrant colors and flavors! It's important that veggie noodles have their own place and are not simply a grain-pasta stand-in. We can enjoy both veggie noodles and traditional pasta! Depending on the style of your spiralizer and the size of the produce you're using, a peeler may work better. Carrots, for example, are too thin for many spiralizers, so a peeler will be more effective for making carrot noodles. If you're using a spiralizer, the easiest ones for little hands have a downward-pushing motion.

DAIRY-FREE, GLUTEN-FREE, NUT-FREE, VEGAN, VEGETARIAN

1 medium yellow squash or zucchini

2 to 3 tablespoons Apple Cider Vinaigrette (page 55) or store-bought dressing

1. **LINE COOK:** Clean the zucchini, using the instructions in the activity (see page 103).

2. **EXECUTIVE CHEF:** Use your spiralizer or peeler to create long, noodle-like strands.

3. **LINE COOK:** Toss with the apple cider vinaigrette and enjoy!

✪ **PLAYTIME!** See who can make the longest noodle! Ask Little Chef: "Can you make one as long as your hand? Your arm? Can you make one that can be worn as a necklace?"

✪ **MIX IT UP:** Try apple spirals with pureed strawberries. Replace the squash with another firm-fleshed fruit or vegetable, like white or sweet potatoes, carrots, cucumbers, broccoli stems, butternut or acorn squash, beets, turnips, radishes, pears, or rhubarb.

Veggie Car Wash

Cleanliness is an important aspect of cooking. Set up a produce washing station to add fun to this valuable concept. This is a great way to keep Little Chef entertained as the cooking process begins. Current recommendations from the FDA advise that soap, including produce-washing liquids, is not recommended for washing vegetables.

MIX IT UP: Increase the fun by using a shoebox to build a carwash-style setup. If you have a train, load the produce on the train and have it deliver the produce to the washing station.

Bucket
Produce washing brush
Produce

1. Fill a bucket with water and give the veggie washing brush to your Little Chef.

2. Have Little Chef wash their hands with soap for 20 seconds.

3. Have Little Chef scrub fruits and veggies.

4. Rinse all produce under running water.

5. Dry produce using a clean towel.

6. Have Little Chef wash their hands with soap for 20 seconds.

Tabbouleh with Fresh Herbs

SERVES 6 · **PREP TIME:** 1 HOUR 30 MINUTES, PLUS UP TO 2 DAYS TO CHILL
COOK TIME: 45 MINUTES

Tabbouleh is a vibrant, delicious salad common in many Middle Eastern countries. Although we often think of salads as lettuce-based, salads look very different around the world. One of the many benefits of this salad is that it tastes better the longer it marinates! Let your salad sit for at least 30 minutes for the flavors to blend and burst. Allowing the ingredients to mingle overnight will yield an even more flavorful dish. The I Spy Delicious Colors! activity following this recipe (page 106) can be done while assembling the salad, or at a different time.

DAIRY-FREE, GLUTEN-FREE OPTIONAL, MESSY HANDS, NUT-FREE, VEGAN, VEGETARIAN

1½ cups water
¾ cup bulgur wheat
1¼ cups small tomatoes, such as Roma
1 medium cucumber
4 green onions
1 bunch parsley
½ bunch fresh mint
⅓ cup olive oil
3 tablespoons lemon juice
1 teaspoon salt
¼ teaspoon freshly ground black pepper

1. **ADULT STEP:** Boil the water in a medium pot. When it comes to a rolling boil, turn off the heat, add the bulgur wheat, and cover. Let sit for 45 minutes or until wheat has softened. Drain off excess liquid and set aside in a large bowl to cool.

2. **EXECUTIVE CHEF:** Seed and dice the tomatoes and dice the cucumber, green onions, parsley, and mint.

3. **LINE COOK:** Add the tomatoes, cucumber, green onions, parsley, and mint to the bowl with the bulgur wheat.

4. **SOUS CHEF:** In a medium bowl, whisk together the olive oil, lemon juice, salt, and pepper.

5. **LINE COOK:** Pour the dressing over the salad and toss well.

6. **ADULT STEP:** Cover the salad and chill in the refrigerator for 30 minutes or as long as 2 days. Enjoy!

✪ **TODDLER SKILLS TIP:** This salad is usually made with diced ingredients, but we never know what Little Chef will end up creating. Aside from the green onions, which may provide too powerful a flavor if left in larger chunks, the salad will be delicious regardless of the size of the individual ingredients.

✪ **MIX IT UP:** Although this salad is traditionally made with bulgur wheat, common variations include couscous or quinoa. Follow the package instructions on your chosen grain (or seed) and proceed with the recipe as written.

I Spy Delicious Colors!

This activity shows one of many ways that kitchen fun can translate into academic success. From the Littlest Chef working on preschool skills to the growing adolescent's grasp of more complex math, the kitchen is a wonderful place to work on academic skills in a delicious and fun setting.

Individual ingredients from Tabbouleh with Fresh Herbs (page 104)

1. Prior to step 3 in the Tabbouleh recipe, take a pause. Examine all the ingredients in front of you with Little Chef.

2. Play "I Spy" with your Little Chef:

   ✿ "I spy something green!"

   ✿ "I spy something little!"

   ✿ "I spy something sour!"

   ✿ "I spy something oily!"

   ✪ **TODDLER SKILLS TIP:**
   Even if Little Chef isn't talking yet, it's valuable to have these conversations. As Little Chef grows, they will have a larger grasp of vocabulary describing taste, texture, and more. This paves the way for increased curiosity and communication, decreasing fear of new foods.

Rainbow Fruit Kebabs with Pineapple Sunrise Dip

MAKES 8 KEBABS • **PREP TIME:** 10 MINUTES

These Rainbow Fruit Kebabs are a fun and delicious snack or side at any time of the day. The action of putting fruit on the kebab skewer helps support fine motor skills for growing chefs. As Little Chef grows, this activity is a wonderful springboard for conversation about colors, numbers, and even weather patterns as you discuss what rainbows are and where they come from! Because traditional skewers have a sharp point, use popsicle sticks or coffee stirrers so you can have fun without the risk.

• •

DAIRY-FREE, GLUTEN-FREE, MESSY HANDS, NUT-FREE, VEGAN, VEGETARIAN

FOR THE PINEAPPLE SUNRISE DIP

½ cup pineapple chunks

½ cup orange juice

1 tablespoon lime Juice

2 to 3 leaves fresh mint

FOR THE RAINBOW FRUIT KEBABS

1 cup strawberries

2 to 3 mandarin oranges

2 bananas

2 kiwis, halved

1 cup grapes, green, red, or mixed (halved for Little Chefs under four years old)

TO MAKE THE PINEAPPLE SUNRISE DIP

1. **LINE COOK:** Add the pineapple, orange juice, lime juice, and mint to a blender and blend until smooth. Set aside.

CONTINUED →

Rainbow Fruit Kebabs with
Pineapple Sunrise Dip CONTINUED

TO MAKE THE RAINBOW FRUIT KEBABS

2. **EXECUTIVE CHEF:** Halve the strawberries, peel and separate the orange segments, peel and cut the bananas into chunks, and scoop and slice the kiwis.

3. **SOUS CHEF:** Thread pieces of fruit onto popsicle sticks or coffee stirrers. Serve with the Pineapple Sunrise Dip.

✪ **MIX IT UP:** If Little Chef is so good at chopping that the chunks can't be skewered effectively, turn their creation into a rainbow fruit salad with pineapple sunrise dressing. You may also want to create a fruit kebab for Little Chef so they can experience the same recipe in two different ways! If Little Chef prefers, switch out the mandarin orange for some fresh pineapple.

✪ **PLAYTIME!** For some extra fun, cut the fruit into shapes before placing them on the skewer using vegetable cutters of your choice. Line Cooks and Sous Chefs can use the hand-over-hand method (page 6) while using cutters, and Executive Chefs can give it a try on their own.

Pineapple Handprint

I t's time to create some delicious art! Pineapple is such a fun fruit. It proudly displays a variety of textures and colors. Use the glorious pineapple as your inspiration for some tasty art in this activity inspired by Arielle Dani Lebovitz, RD.

Pineapple Sunrise Dip (page 107)

Piece of white or light-colored paper

OPTION 1

1. Use Little Chef's whole palm to make a fun pineapple handprint by dipping it in dressing and pressing it onto a piece of paper.

OPTION 2

2. Create a beautiful pineapple by using multiple thumbprints on paper.

⭐ **MIX IT UP:** Use a variety of dressings and dips (page 94) to create a rainbow, a tree, or portraits of each other!

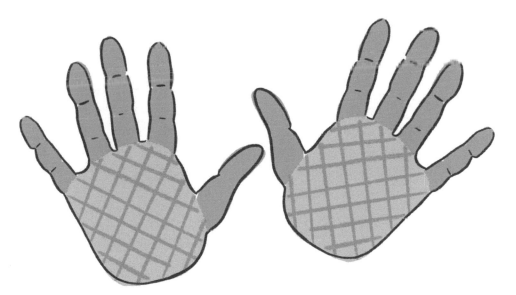

Colorful Mixed Bean Salad

SERVES 6 · **PREP TIME:** 15 MINUTES

Beans are often overlooked as an amazing kid food, but the variety in color, size, and shape brings a fun, multisensory experience to the table.

....

DAIRY-FREE, GLUTEN-FREE, MESSY HANDS, NUT-FREE, VEGAN, VEGETARIAN

2 tablespoons cilantro, fresh

⅓ cup red onion, cut in half

1 medium avocado

1 (14½-ounce) can black beans or 15 ounces cooked black beans

1 cup corn niblets, fresh or frozen

1 cup edamame

1 garlic clove, minced

½ cup cherry tomatoes, halved

⅓ cup olive oil

2 teaspoons lime zest

½ cup lime juice

1 teaspoon kosher salt

....

1. **LINE COOK:** Wash the cilantro well in a wash bucket (see page 103) and then rinse under running water.

2. **EXECUTIVE CHEF** (with assistance): Roll the cilantro up into a torpedo and slice. Repeat until the cilantro is roughly chopped. Set aside.

3. **EXECUTIVE CHEF:** Using goggles (page 57), dice the onion and set aside.

4. **ADULT STEP:** Cut the avocado in half and remove the pit.

5. **EXECUTIVE CHEF:** Using a butter knife or toddler knife, score the avocado flesh by cutting vertical and horizontal lines in a hashtag pattern; then use a spoon to scoop it into a medium mixing bowl.

6. **LINE COOK:** Add the cilantro, onion, black beans, corn, edamame, garlic, and tomatoes to the mixing bowl and stir.

7. **SOUS CHEF:** In a small bowl, combine the oil, lime zest, lime juice, and salt. Stir or cover and shake.

8. **LINE COOK:** Pour the dressing over the salad, mix well, and enjoy!

✪ **TODDLER SKILLS TIP:** If you have a garlic press, show Little Chef how it works! The squeezing motion is fun, but seeing the pressed garlic come out the other side just might be the highlight of this recipe. For more fun, show Little Chef how you can use the garlic press for mincing ginger or even for smashing egg yolks for deviled eggs!

✪ **PLAYTIME!** Instead of buying shelled edamame, buy the full pod and show Little Chef how much fun it is to shoot the beans out of the pod! Can you play Edamame Football?

Have You Bean Counting?

Beans are so versatile and nutritious and are a staple in many different types of dishes from all around the world. They are also a great tool for those learning colors, if you use two or more types of beans, or those learning how to count. This activity is listed in order of skill level so Little Chef can progress as they grow. Experiment and see where this game takes you! Be sure to cook the beans before you start the activity, because dried beans are a choking hazard.

....

1 cup cooked beans, such as garbanzo beans, red or white kidney beans, or lima beans

....

1. Count out the beans together. Can you count to 5? 10?

2. Can you make a happy face? How many beans are in the happy face?

3. Can you make a circle out of 15 beans? 20?

4. Can you create the first letter of your name?

5. As Little Chef grows, keep asking them questions. Consider:

   ✿ If I have 10 beans and you take 3, how many beans do I have left?

   ✿ How many beans are in a cup of beans?

   ✿ Can you count beans in another language?

Sweet and Savory Roasted Brussels Sprouts

SERVES 6 • **PREP TIME:** 15 MINUTES • **COOK TIME:** 45 MINUTES

Brussels sprouts are just one of those foods that somehow got a reputation for being *the worst*, along with lima beans and liver and onions. That may be due to the bitter, smooshy, slimy experience when they are boiled. However, roasted vegetables take on a sweet and savory flavor that keeps you coming back for more. Introduce Little Chef to the fun they can have with Brussels sprouts in this recipe.

....

DAIRY-FREE, GLUTEN-FREE, MESSY HANDS, NUT-FREE, VEGAN, VEGETARIAN

1 pound fresh Brussels sprouts

1 large sweet potato

2 garlic cloves, diced

⅓ cup olive oil, plus more for spraying the baking sheet

¼ teaspoon cumin

1 teaspoon salt

Freshly ground black pepper

Juice of 1 lemon

Pinch fresh thyme, for garnish (optional)

....

1. **ADULT STEP:** Preheat the oven to 400°F.

2. **ADULT STEP:** Trim the Brussels sprouts by cutting off the little brown end and discarding any yellow leaves. Cut in halves or quarters.

3. **EXECUTIVE CHEF:** Peel the sweet potato.

4. **ADULT STEP:** Cut the sweet potato in half lengthwise.

5. **EXECUTIVE CHEF:** Chop the sweet potato into roughly one-inch-size pieces.

CONTINUED →

Sweet and Savory Roasted Brussels Sprouts
CONTINUED

6. **SOUS CHEF:** Add the chopped sweet potatoes and Brussels sprouts to a large mixing bowl; then add the garlic, oil, cumin, and salt and season with pepper. Stir well.

7. **EXECUTIVE CHEF:** Line a baking sheet with foil and spray with olive oil.

8. **LINE COOK** (with assistance): Pour the veggies onto the baking sheet in one layer.

9. **ADULT STEP:** Roast for 40 to 45 minutes until brown or until a fork will easily slide into the veggies.

10. **ADULT STEP:** Let cool until the vegetables reach an acceptable temperature for Little Chef.

11. **SOUS CHEF:** Place the veggies in a bowl and toss with the lemon juice and garnish with fresh thyme (if using).

✪ **TODDLER SKILLS TIP:** In order to cut effectively, any round ingredients must be halved lengthwise to provide a safe and secure experience for Little Chef. Place the flat side on the cutting board so the ingredient does not move around as Little Chef chops.

✪ **NUTRITION TIP:** This recipe is full of fiber that not only helps things move along smoothly, but helps give a satisfying, full feeling. This dish is nearly a meal all on its own, but you can round it out by serving it alongside a protein-based dish.

Bowling with Brussels

Bowling has been a popular pastime since ancient Egypt in 5000 BCE! In this version, inspired by Arielle Dani Lebovitz, RD, we bring it down to Little Chef's level with a much lighter ball—the Brussels sprout!

Support stand (books or toys)

Table

Plank (book, cardboard, or light piece of wood)

Pins (cardboard tubes such as toilet paper rolls or creatively cut jicama or other veggie)

Brussels sprouts

⭐ **MIX IT UP:** Experiment with ramp height! Does the "ball" move faster or slower? Are the pins easier to knock down if they are closer or farther away?

1. On top of your table, stack books or toys until they are 3 inches or higher.

2. Lay one end of your plank on top of the stack with the other end directly on the table.

3. Set up your pins, bowling alley–style.

4. Roll the Brussels sprout from the top of the ramp down to the pins and see how many you can knock down!

Fruit and
Yogurt Parfait
with Granola
PAGE 118
▼

▲
Fruit
Puppets
PAGE 120

CHAPTER SIX

Diving into Desserts

Fruit and Yogurt Parfait with Granola

SERVES 6 · **PREP TIME:** 15 MINUTES · **COOK TIME:** 55 MINUTES

Homemade granola is simple, delicious, and a tasty way to start or end the day! Mix up the add-ins to make your own perfect granola: slivered almonds, sunflower seeds, freeze-dried fruit, well-chopped nuts, and hemp hearts make flavorful additions.

....

DAIRY-FREE OPTIONAL, GLUTEN-FREE OPTIONAL, MESSY HANDS, NUT-FREE OPTIONAL, VEGAN OPTIONAL, VEGETARIAN

8 Medjool dates, pitted

3 cups water

3 cups old-fashioned oats

1 cup unsweetened shredded coconut

1 cup mixed slivered almonds and shelled sunflower seeds

½ teaspoon salt

½ cup coconut oil

1 teaspoon vanilla

¼ cup nut or seed butter

¼ cup raspberries

2 large strawberries

½ large banana

¼ cup plain Greek yogurt or non-dairy alternative

....

1. **ADULT STEP:** Boil the dates in the water for 5 minutes, or soak in warm water for 2 to 3 hours; then blend in a blender or food processor until smooth.

2. **ADULT STEP:** Preheat the oven to 300°F.

3. **LINE COOK:** Mix the oats, shredded coconut, almonds and seeds, and salt in a large mixing bowl.

4. **LINE COOK:** Add the coconut oil, vanilla, date puree, and nut or seed butter to the dry ingredients and mix well.

5. **EXECUTIVE CHEF:** Prepare a baking sheet by lining it with parchment paper.

6. **LINE COOK:** Spread the granola mix evenly on the prepared baking sheet.

7. **ADULT STEP:** Bake for about 50 minutes, stirring every 15 minutes until the mixture starts to brown; then remove from the oven and let cool completely.

8. **SOUS CHEF:** Wash and dry the berries and slice the banana.

9. **LINE COOK:** Layer the yogurt, fruit, and granola in a clear cup. Enjoy!

✪ **TODDLER SKILLS TIP:** When selecting add-ins, be sure to keep in mind choking hazards for Little Chef (page 9).

✪ **MIX IT UP:** Granola can be so versatile. The writers at SuperHealthyKids.com suggest some of these really fun ways to eat it: Use it as a muffin topping. Use it to top baked apples. Roll bananas in granola. Add it to your oatmeal. Add warm milk and enjoy as a comforting breakfast. Wrap it up nicely and gift it to a friend!

Fruit Puppets

There is nothing like getting to know your food on another level. Give your fruit a voice with a fun puppet show! Ask your fruit puppet about its favorite food, hobby, dreams, or even career goals.

Popsicle sticks

Chunks of varied fruits

1. Use a wooden popsicle stick as a body and a chunk of fruit as the head of the puppet.

2. Have puppets interact with each other!

✪ **MIX IT UP:** You can keep this very basic or create a whole context for your fruit puppets. Use a cardboard box to create a stage and involve fun props! Get some self-adhesive googly eyes, stick them to the skin of a fruit or vegetable, and see where your imagination takes you.

Tropical Blended Popsicles

MAKES 6 (2-OUNCE) POPSICLES · **PREP TIME:** 15 MINUTES, PLUS 4 TO 6 HOURS TO FREEZE

Popsicles are refreshing, tasty, and so easy to make. Little Chef will love adding ingredients to the blender and then enjoying the final product on a hot summer day—or on a rainy day for that matter! Smaller kids enjoy immediate gratification and don't understand the concept of making something for later, so be sure to give Little Chef a sample before it goes in the freezer.

DAIRY-FREE OPTIONAL, GLUTEN-FREE, MESSY HANDS, NUT-FREE OPTIONAL, VEGAN OPTIONAL, VEGETARIAN

✪ **MIX IT UP:** You can make a standard frozen treat on a stick, or you can change it up with a push-up pop. Even create delicious ice cubes to make your water more interesting. Tropical ice balls will keep your melon ball salad cold and refreshing!

1 mango
1 banana
4 ounces guava nectar
½ cup pineapple chunks

1. **ADULT STEP:** Cut the mango in half. Leaving the skin on, cut vertical and horizontal slashes into the mango flesh, creating a hashtag pattern. Push on the skin so the scored mango flesh pops outward.

2. **LINE COOK:** With a spoon, scoop the mango out of the skin and place in the blender.

3. **LINE COOK** (with assistance): Place the banana, guava nectar, and pineapple chunks in the blender and puree until smooth. If mixture is too thick, add 1 tablespoon of water at a time until it blends nicely.

4. **ADULT STEP** (with assistance from **LINE COOK**): Pour the mixture into a popsicle mold until full, put the lid on, and freeze for 4 to 6 hours.

Be a Popsicle

Feeling a little bit prickly? Get out of your skin and pretend to be a pineapple popsicle!

● ●

⚙ **TODDLER SKILLS TIP:**
Let this activity go where it takes you. Little Chef has a growing imagination that can be supported through imaginary play. Participating in fun play along with Little Chef helps strengthen their self-confidence.

**Tropical Blended
Popsicle** (page 121)

● ●

1. Sample your popsicle or popsicle juice and pretend to turn into a popsicle!

2. Ask your child some questions about being a popsicle:

   ✿ What shape are you?

   ✿ What color are you?

   ✿ How do you taste?

   ✿ How do you melt?

Peanut Butter Snowball Bites

MAKES ABOUT 15 BITES · **PREP TIME:** 5 MINUTES, PLUS 10 MINUTES TO COOL

These delicious bites look like little snowballs, and in one of my cooking classes, we created little snowmen out of these energy bites, with scarves and all! This is a fun food to make with Little Chef, and it's also packed full of nutrition, including fiber, protein, and omega-3s. But, of course, the most important ingredient is the smile on Little Chef's face. Old-fashioned oats work best with this recipe—instant oats fall apart.

DAIRY-FREE, GLUTEN-FREE OPTIONAL, MESSY HANDS, NUT-FREE OPTIONAL, VEGAN OPTIONAL, VEGETARIAN

1 cup old-fashioned oats

3 tablespoons honey or maple syrup

¼ cup unsweetened shredded coconut, plus more for rolling

½ cup plus 2 tablespoons peanut butter, sunflower seed butter, or cashew butter

¼ cup flax meal

⅓ cup mixed unsweetened dried berries and finely chopped nuts

1. **LINE COOK:** Combine the oats, honey, coconut, nut butter, flax meal, and berries and nuts in a large mixing bowl.

2. **ADULT STEP:** Refrigerate for 10 minutes.

3. **SOUS CHEF:** Take a tablespoon-sized amount and roll it into a ball, pressing the ingredients together.

4. **LINE COOK:** Roll balls in coconut to coat.

CONTINUED →

Peanut Butter Snowball Bites CONTINUED

✪ **TODDLER SKILLS TIP:**
Refrigerating the ingredients
in step 2 is advised because
the ingredients will hold
together better after getting
to know each other in a chilly
environment. But if Little
Chef is anxious and wants to
get rolling, skipping the step
won't be a problem. Just be
sure to refrigerate any leftover snowballs in a covered
container to prevent them
from falling apart.

✪ **NUTRITION TIP:** Peanut,
sunflower seed, or cashew
butter will work nicely in this
recipe, but almond butter
is too thin to hold the bites
together. Be sure to use a
thick nut or seed butter for
the best result.

Measuring Big and Small

Measuring is fantastic for sneaky academics. As Little Chef plays with oats, shredded coconut, and flax meal, they don't know they are also learning numbers, colors, and even basic fractions!

1 cup old-fashioned oats

¼ cup shredded coconut

⅓ cup unsweetened dried berries, chopped dried fruit, or finely chopped nuts

Selection of measuring cups and spoons

⭐ **TODDLER SKILLS TIP:**
This activity can grow with Little Chef. Before you know it, you'll be discussing how many half cups are in a whole cup or how to triple a recipe! You'll discuss how the sweet honey and the savory nut butter serve to bind the ingredients together and how coconuts grow.

1. Measure out the ingredients.

2. Ask Little Chef some questions about measuring:

✿ How many tablespoons are in a cup?

✿ Do you have more oats or more coconut?

✿ Which ingredient is the heaviest? The lightest?

✿ Which ingredient tastes the best? This can be answered in theory or after tasting different ingredients.

Frozen Yogurt Bark

SERVES 6 · **PREP TIME:** 15 MINUTES, PLUS 2 TO 4 HOURS TO FREEZE

Yogurt is known for its health benefits. Healthy fats support brain growth and development, and the probiotics are wonderful for gut health and immunity. This colorful dish easily doubles as a snack or a dessert, and even the tiniest hands can take the lead. Be sure to keep your yogurt spread thin so you can break and eat.

....

DAIRY-FREE OPTIONAL, GLUTEN-FREE, MESSY HANDS, NUT-FREE OPTIONAL, VEGAN OPTIONAL, VEGETARIAN

✪ **NUTRITION TIP:** Greek yogurt is known to be higher in protein and calcium, but do you know why? It's the straining process! Whey, a milk protein, is strained out of the yogurt, condensing what's left and giving it that smooth and creamy feel that is so satisfying.

✪ **MIX IT UP:** Make this recipe into a popsicle by combining all the ingredients, mixing well, and freezing in popsicle molds overnight.

2 cups full-fat Greek yogurt (or non-dairy alternative)

2 tablespoons maple syrup

½ teaspoon vanilla extract

½ cup toppings, such as sliced strawberries, blueberries, shredded coconut, dark chocolate shavings, finely chopped cranberries or raisins, crushed nuts, hulled hemp seeds, ½ teaspoon lemon zest

....

1. **SOUS CHEF:** Mix the yogurt, maple syrup, and vanilla extract in a small mixing bowl.

2. **EXECUTIVE CHEF:** Line a baking tray with wax paper.

3. **ADULT STEP** (with assistance from Little Chef): Pour the yogurt mix onto the prepared baking tray and spread evenly, ideally not thicker than ½ inch at any point.

4. **LINE COOK:** Sprinkle your chosen toppings over the yogurt.

5. **ADULT STEP:** Place in the freezer for 2 to 4 hours until hard; then use a sharp knife to break the bark into pieces. Enjoy!

Create an Ice Cream Stand or Ice Cream Truck!

Many of us have fond memories of hanging out in front of the house with a lemonade stand, trying to get the attention of neighborhood drivers and pedestrians with the hope of earning a quarter for the piggy bank. Bring this concept up to speed with an ice cream truck in your very own house. Get creative with what's around you and have a blast!

1. Make delicious Frozen Yogurt Bark (page 126).

2. While it's in the freezer, use materials around the house to create an ice cream stand or ice cream truck.

3. Pretend with each other or invite friends to join the party!

⭐ **TODDLER SKILLS TIP:** Involve Little Chef in the design of the stand or truck by asking open-ended questions: What color do you think our truck should be? Where would our truck be parked? How much should we charge for a piece of yogurt bark? Be prepared for some fun answers!

Chocolate Fruit Tacos

MAKES 16 TACOS • **PREP TIME:** 20 MINUTES

Inspired by SheKnows.com, this sweet twist on a classic is sure to become part of your regular rotation. Try different combinations, such as banana and chocolate hazelnut spread or mango and shredded coconut.

....

DAIRY-FREE, GLUTEN-FREE OPTIONAL, MESSY HANDS, NUT-FREE OPTIONAL, VEGAN OPTIONAL, VEGETARIAN

1 cup whole-wheat flour

3 cups all-purpose flour

1 teaspoon baking powder

¼ teaspoon salt

⅓ cup cocoa powder

⅓ cup coconut oil (or light-tasting olive or avocado oil or melted butter)

4 tablespoons honey or maple syrup

1½ cups warm water

1 cup strawberries or 1 medium banana

½ cup nut or seed butter

....

1. **LINE COOK:** Mix the flours, baking powder, salt, and cocoa powder together in a large bowl.

2. **SOUS CHEF:** Add the oil, honey, and warm water to the bowl and mix until a large ball of dough is formed.

3. **EXECUTIVE CHEF**, alternating with **ADULT STEP** (see page 14): Knead the dough on a floured surface for 4 to 5 minutes.

4. **EXECUTIVE CHEF:** Cut the ball in half and then in half again. Continue until you have 16 small dough balls.

5. **ADULT STEP:** Cover and let the dough rest for 10 minutes.

6. **EXECUTIVE CHEF:** Place a ball of dough between two sheets of wax paper and roll out to form a circle that is ¼ inch thick and about 5 inches across. Repeat with all 16 balls.

7. **ADULT STEP:** Heat a dry skillet over medium heat or heat an electric griddle to 300°F. Cook about 30 seconds on each side. Set aside to cool.

8. **EXECUTIVE CHEF:** Wash and slice the strawberries or chop the banana.

9. **SOUS CHEF:** Spread nut or seed butter on a tortilla, add fruit, and fold into a taco shape.

✪ **TODDLER SKILLS TIP:** If you are using an electric griddle, your Executive Chef can help by placing the raw tortilla on the griddle and flipping it. An electric griddle provides a more stable surface, making it safer for Little Chef to help confidently. Of course, supervision is a must for this step.

✪ **NUTRITION TIP:** We associate chocolate with decadence, but it's actually full of nutrition! Chocolate is a powerful source of antioxidants, which support the immune system and heart health.

Flavor Plate

My kids love sweets, and so do I! But as I'm always telling them, there are five different types of flavors, and it's important to experience all of them daily. That's my fancy way of saying, "No, we are not having ice cream for lunch." This flavor plate helps Little Chef understand what those five flavors are and how we can have fun experiencing new taste sensations.

Plate

One food item representing each of the five flavors:

- **Sweet: honey or maple syrup**
- **Salty: a pinch of salt, soy sauce, or salted cracker**
- **Sour: lemon juice, a small piece of citrus rind, or plain yogurt**
- **Bitter: a pinch of cocoa powder**
- **Umami: broth, fish, or mushrooms (mushroom powder)**

1. Place a small amount of each ingredient on the plate, keeping each item separate.

2. Take a small taste of each item and discuss the flavor. How do you like it? Would you eat it again?

⭐ **MIX IT UP:** If you have the ingredients on hand, make a couple of different plates and discuss the different experiences.

✪ **NUTRITION TIP:** We have taste receptors all over the tongue and on the roof of the mouth. If Little Chef is excited by this activity, test out the theory! Can you taste salt on the tip of the tongue? Or sweet on the side? Does one side of the tongue seem more sensitive to a particular flavor?

Measurement Conversions

VOLUME EQUIVALENTS (LIQUID)

US Standard	US Standard (ounces)	Metric (approximate)
2 tablespoons	1 fl. oz.	30 mL
¼ cup	2 fl. oz.	60 mL
½ cup	4 fl. oz.	120 mL
1 cup	8 fl. oz.	240 mL
1½ cups	12 fl. oz.	355 mL
2 cups or 1 pint	16 fl. oz.	475 mL
4 cups or 1 quart	32 fl. oz.	1 L
1 gallon	128 fl. oz.	4 L

OVEN TEMPERATURES

Fahrenheit (F)	Celsius (C) (approximate)
250°F	120°C
300°F	150°C
325°F	165°C
350°F	180°C
375°F	190°C
400°F	200°C
425°F	220°C
450°F	230°C

VOLUME EQUIVALENTS (DRY)

US Standard	Metric (approximate)
⅛ teaspoon	0.5 mL
¼ teaspoon	1 mL
½ teaspoon	2 mL
¾ teaspoon	4 mL
1 teaspoon	5 mL
1 tablespoon	15 mL
¼ cup	59 mL
⅓ cup	79 mL
½ cup	118 mL
⅔ cup	156 mL
¾ cup	177 mL
1 cup	235 mL
2 cups or 1 pint	475 mL
3 cups	700 mL
4 cups or 1 quart	1 L

WEIGHT EQUIVALENTS

US Standard	Metric (approximate)
½ ounce	15 g
1 ounce	30 g
2 ounces	60 g
4 ounces	115 g
8 ounces	225 g
12 ounces	340 g
16 ounces or 1 pound	455 g

Resources

Nutrition for Raising Children

✿ **BabyBloomNutrition.com/Nap-Time-Nutrition:** Free and relevant information on parenting, children, and nutrition. Use the search tab or playlists to explore topics covered since 2016, including gluten, fat, pumping, how to read growth charts, and so much more!

✿ *Beyond a Bite: Activities for a Mindful Mealtime* by Yaffi Lvova, RDN

✿ **ExperienceDeliciousNow.com:** Arielle Dani Lebovitz's growing collection of food-based art books and freebies.

Food Introduction Resources

✿ *Stage-by-Stage Baby Food Cookbook* by Yaffi Lvova, RDN

✿ **FeedingLittles.com:** Feeding Littles has wonderful online courses on both baby-led weaning and toddler feeding. Check BabyBloomNutrition.com /additional-support and for sales or discount codes!

Child Nutrition Resources

✿ **EllynSatterInstitute.org:** Ellyn Satter, MS, RD, MSSW, developed the division of responsibility in feeding model. Her site is a valuable resource for further information on guiding your child toward a healthy relationship with food and body.

✿ **FeedingBytes.com:** Natalia Stasenko, RD, is a feeding expert who provides up-to-date and convenient resources on her website and social media outlets.

✿ **TheFeedingDoctor.com:** Katja Rowell, MD, provides books, blogs, and other free resources on child nutrition, extreme picky eating, food preoccupation, and much more.

✿ **HealthyChildren.org:** The American Academy of Pediatrics' parenting website provides reliable health information about children and parenting.

✿ **YourFeedingTeam.com:** Natalia Stasenko, Jo Cormack, and Simone Emery team up to provide guidance for parents overcoming picky eating obstacles.

Nutrition for the Sensory Sensitive Child

✿ *Beyond a Bite Special Edition: Sensory Food Exploration for the Neurodivergent Population* by Yaffi Lvova, RDN, and Hana Eichele, MOT, OTR/L

✿ **NaureenHunani.com:** Naureen Hunani, RD, is a feeding therapist specializing in autism. She offers individual counseling and parent workshops.

✿ **RootsPediatricTherapy.com:** Hana Eichele, MOT, OTR/L, is an occupational therapist and feeding therapist focused on helping parents identify underlying stress and developmental concerns.

Babywearing Resources

✿ **OnyaBaby.com/blogs/go-anywhere/find-a-local-babywearing-group:** A resource for finding a local babywearing group.

✿ **TandemTrouble.com:** LaKeta Kemp, babywearing coach and mom of twins (like me!), demonstrates how to safely and comfortably wear twins.

Breastfeeding Resources

✿ **CrystalKarges.com** and **MamaandSweetPeaNutrition.com:** Find reliable and compassionate advice on breastfeeding and breastfeeding nutrition from these two registered dietitians.

✿ **ILCA.org:** The International Lactation Consultant Association has a search function to connect you with an international board-certified lactation consultant. Having an advocate during this time can provide important relief.

Baby Sleep Resource

✿ **GetQuietNights.com:** Tracy Spackman provides gentle sleep coaching information. See her blog for daily schedules with alternative options.

Toddler Cooking Resources

✿ **IKEA Hack:** Toddler Learning Tower Stool
at happygreylucky.com/ikea-hack-toddler-learning-tower-stool

✿ **pinterest.com/yaffi/boards:** For specific products I love, check out my Pinterest boards!

References

Alter-Rasche, Deborah. "Painting with Seasoning and Spices. Sensory Creativity." *Learn with Play at Home*. August 7, 2012. learnwithplayathome.com/2012/08/painting-with-seasoning-and-spices.html.

Bongiorno, Laurel. "10 Things Every Parent Should Know About Play." National Association for the Education of Young Children. Accessed September 12, 2020. naeyc.org/our-work/families/10-things-every-parent-play.

"CDC's Developmental Milestones." Centers for Disease Control and Prevention. June 10, 2020. cdc.gov/ncbddd/actearly/milestones.

Chicot, Rebecca. "Why Does My Toddler Hate Mess?" *Essential Parent*. Accessed September 12, 2020. essentialparent.com/lesson/why-does-my-toddler-hate-mess-1969.

Coe, Andrew. *Chop Suey: A Cultural History of Chinese Food in the United States*. New York: Oxford University Press, 2009.

Craftulate. "Use Herbs and Spices to Scent and Colour This Homemade All Natural Play Dough!" *Craftulate*. March 17, 2020. craftulate.com/homemade-herb-and-spice-play-dough.

Duvinage, Sina. "Ikea Hack: Toddler Learning Tower Stool." *Happy Grey Lucky*. March 30, 2017. happygreylucky.com/ikea-hack-toddler-learning-tower-stool.

Ehrenberg, S., L. A. Leone, B. Sharpe, K. Reardon, and S. Anzman-Frasca. "Using Repeated Exposure Through Hands-on Cooking to Increase Children's Preferences for Fruits and Vegetables." *Appetite* 142 (November 2019).

The Ellen Satter Institute. Accessed September 15, 2020. ellynsatterinstitute.org.

Monson, Natalie. "Granola: 14 Ways to Use It." *Super Healthy Kids*. April 12, 2019. superhealthykids.com/parenting/14-ways-to-use-granola.

Moyses, Kendra. "Movement Can Increase Learning in Children." *MSU Extension*. Michigan State University. October 3, 2018. canr.msu.edu/news/movement_can_increase_learning_in_children.

Mullen, Kris. "Breakfast Tacos Are Good, but Fruit Breakfast Tacos Are Better." SheKnows. July 10, 2018. sheknows.com/food-and-recipes/articles/961851 /fruit-tacos-with-chocolate-tortillas-recipe.

My Gym Maitland. "7 Benefits of Forward Rolls." August 13, 2014. mygymmaitland.wordpress.com/2014/08/13/7-benefits-of-forward-rolls.

Perry, Lynn K., et al. "Highchair Philosophers: The Impact of Seating Context-Dependent Exploration on Children's Naming Biases." *Wiley Online Library* December 1, 2013. onlinelibrary.wiley.com/doi/abs/10.1111/desc.12147.

"Reading and Storytelling with Babies and Children." *Raising Children Network*. June 22, 2018. raisingchildren.net.au/babies/play-learning/literacy -reading-stories/reading-storytelling.

Schoenberger, Jenni. "DIY Color Bubbles." Mama Plus One. March 9, 2015. mamaplusone.com/diy-color-bubbles.

Stasenko, Natalia, et al. "Exposure or Pressure." Your Feeding Team. Instagram, July 20, 2020. instagram.com/p/CC3uoRYptM1/.

Thompson, Anna. Food Explorers Kids. Instagram, 2020. instagram.com /food_explorers_kids.

US Food and Drug Administration, Office of the Commissioner. "7 Tips for Cleaning Fruits, Vegetables." 2018. fda.gov/consumers/consumer-updates /7-tips-cleaning-fruits-vegetables.

Wei, Marylynn. "More Than Just a Game: Yoga for School-Age Children." *Harvard Health Blog*. Harvard Medical School. June 24, 2020. health.harvard.edu/blog/more-than-just-a-game-yoga-for-school-age -children-201601299055.

Wu, Steph. "Playing with Your Food Is Actually Good for You." *Kidspot Australia*. July 3, 2017. kidspot.com.au/parenting/child/child -behaviour/playing-with-your-food-is-actually-good-for-you/news-story /ee7362d08893bc6599bcff364c4718ee.

Index

Acknowledgments

For Joan and Lenny Kalmenson and Dina and Arkadiy Lvov, who drew on generations of knowledge to pass along a love of food, culture, and exploration.

To the Lev of my life, who holds my hand on this journey. And finally, to our children—Shimon, Benjamin, and Daniel—who will continue that adventure.

I would also like to thank those who helped this book become a reality: Laura Apperson; Bracha Kopstick, RD; and everyone else on the Callisto team.

About the Author

Yaffi Lvova, RDN, is a Registered Dietitian Nutritionist and owner of Baby Bloom Nutrition®. She holds degrees in both Comparative Religions and Nutrition and Dietetics from Arizona State University.

After a difficult journey toward and into motherhood, Yaffi became mother to twins, plus one, and used her experience and clinical knowledge to shift gears, providing nutrition education to new and expecting parents and helping smooth the transition into parenthood.

In 2015, Yaffi created Toddler Test Kitchen™ (ToddlerTestKitchen.net) with immense help from Claudine Wessel, LaKeta Kemp, and Sarah Garone. This unique culinary adventure puts small children in the driver's seat—or at the cutting board, as it were—helping to bolster their self-esteem and feed their curiosity by creating something delicious!

In 2016, Yaffi went live with a weekly Facebook segment and subsequent podcast, Nap Time Nutrition (NapTimeNutrition.com), covering all topics parenthood and nutrition.

In 2019, Yaffi was brought on board for the update of *Discover Mindful Eating for Kids* with Megrette Fletcher.

In 2020, Yaffi published *Stage-By-Stage Baby Food Cookbook* and *Beyond a Bite: Activities for a Mindful Mealtime*

In 2021, Yaffi published *Beyond a Bite Neurodiverse Edition: Joyful Activities for Sensory Food Exploration*.

You can find Yaffi at BabyBloomNutrition.com. On Facebook she is @BabyBloomNutrition and @ToddlerTestKitchenAZ. On Instagram you can find her at @toddler.testkitchen. On Twitter, she is Yaffi Lvova @BabyBloomNutrit.

CPSIA information can be obtained
at www.ICGtesting.com
Printed in the USA
BVHW092148121021
618542BV00002B/3